STUDIES IN TH

Inflation and UK monetary policy

David F. Heathfield
University of Southampton

and

Mark Russell
Lord Wandsworth College

Series Editor
Bryan Hurl
Harrow School

To Ivor Pearce, teacher and friend

Heinemann Educational Publishers
Halley Court, Jordan Hill, Oxford OX2 8EJ
a division of Reed Educational & Professional Publishing Ltd

MADRID   ATHENS   PARIS
FLORENCE   PRAGUE   WARSAW
PORTSMOUTH NH (USA)   CHICAGO   SAO PAULO
SINGAPORE   TOKYO   MELBOURNE   AUCKLAND
IBADAN   GABORONE   JOHANNESBURG

First published as *UK inflation*, 1992
Revised edition published 1996

99   98   97   96
10 9 8 7 6 5 4 3 2 1

British Library Cataloguing in Publication Data
A catalogue record for this book is available from the British Library

ISBN 0 435 33035 7

Typeset and illustrated by TechType, Abingdon, Oxon.
Printed and bound in Great Britain by Clays Ltd, St Ives plc.

Acknowledgements

The publishers would like to thank the following for the use of copyright material:
Associated Examining Board for the questions on pp. 40, 50, 57, 69–71; Bank of England for the figure on p. 14 and the adapted report on pp. 81–2; Barclays Bank for the figure on p. 76; Alan Budd for the quotation on p. 83; the Central Statistical Office for the data in the figures on p. 41. (adapted from Annual Abstract of Statistics, 1994 (Crown Copyright, 1994); published by HMSO), the figures on p. 49 and for the extract quoted on pp. 57–8; © *The Economist* 1994 for the cartoon and extract on p. 20; Newspaper Publishing plc for the extract from the *Independent on Sunday* on p. 32; Northern Examinations and Assessment Board for the questions on pp. 24, 80–1; Oxford and Cambridge Schools Examination Board for the questions on pp. 88–9; the Institute of Economic Affairs for the article on pp. 88–9; *The Observer* for the article on pp. 70–1; Sterling Books for the figure on p. 51; © Times Newspapers Ltd for the figures from *The Times* on pp. 50–1; University of Cambridge Local Examinations Syndicate on pp. 15–17, 24, 87; University of London Examinations and Assessment Council on pp. 15–6, 24, 50–2, 57–8, 69, 80–1, 88; University of Oxford Delegacy of Local Examinations on pp. 24, 40–2, 69, 80–1, 88.
The publishers have made every attempt to contact the correct copyright holders. However, if any material has been incorrectly attributed, we will be happy to correct this at the earliest opportunity.

Contents

Preface

In this new edition the opportunity is taken to introduce monetary policy explicitly as the anvil on which inflation goals are fashioned. The previous edition has been extensively rewritten and extended to keep its lead position in economic theory and applied economics, post-ERM, for the new A and AS levels.

Bryan Hurl
Series Editor

Acknowledgements

This book has benefited greatly from the observations and guidance of the Series Editor, Bryan Hurl. A number of present and former students have assisted us in making this a more readable and accurate volume by commenting on earlier drafts, preparing graphs and offering welcome support. Our thanks to James Cranswick, James Currie, Paul Lewis, Jon Palmer, Hall Smith, William Tovey, Colin Walker and Tim Woolfson. Any remaining errors are, of course, our own.

DFH and MCR, October 1995

Introduction

This book tackles the area of economics that is perhaps least well understood by both teachers and students. Inflation is a well-known phenomenon, but much of the evidence about recent inflation is in dispute. Monetary policy is an area that has undergone many changes since the breakdown in 1971 of the fixed exchange rate regime known as the Bretton Woods system.

The changes in the conduct and theory of monetary policy have left many non-specialists behind. The problem of understanding monetary policy has been made worse by the technical nature of the economic theory behind policy, and by the willingness of the press and politicians to label *all* policies monetarist or Keynesian. In this slim volume it would be difficult to avoid using convenient labels, and impossible to try to explain all of the very complex sub-plots; we do, however, try to offer A level students an insight into the way monetary policy is being conducted. It is, after all, the area of greatest interest to the non-specialist and affects the lives of everyone in the country.

Chapter 1 discusses the meaning of the term inflation and *Chapter 2* details how inflation is measured. *Chapter 3* looks at the costs and benefits of inflation to society and questions whether inflation is always a bad thing.

In *Chapter 4* we look at the conflicting views on the causes of inflation. As in many areas of economics there is controversy here, and in *Chapter 5* the student is given the chance to assess the evidence in support of the conflicting theories. Some of our students found Chapter 5 annoying because it reached no neat conclusion, but the jury is still out on the question of who is right, and the controversy continues!

In *Chapter 6* we discuss the financial system, and particularly the ability of banks to create credit. *Chapter 7* then continues to explain the theory of monetary policy, while *Chapter 8* explains that theory and reality have only occasionally met.

Chapter 9 is entitled 'Looking forward'. It tries to look forward to the possible changes that will occur in monetary policy in the next few years. Students are encouraged to remember that monetary policy evolves on an almost daily basis, and they should follow carefully the pronouncements of the Chancellor of the Exchequer and Governor of the Bank of England as their course progresses.

In line with the **new SCAA Core Subject requirements** introduced by all boards from 1995, the book uses aggregate demand and aggregate supply analysis rather than the more traditional Keynesian income–expenditure approach. For those unfamiliar with this analysis, references are provided.

The book is designed to cover the needs of those taking either the traditional 'linear' A levels, as offered by all of the examination boards, or the new modular A levels. Those taking the UCLES modular course will find that the book covers the appropriate material for the National Economy module, and also the Financial Economics module.

Chapter One

Defining inflation

'Inflation means that your money won't buy as much today as it did when you didn't have any.' (Anon)

What is inflation?

Inflation today is taken to mean a *sustained rise in the aggregate, or general, price level.*

The experience of the 1970s, when inflation reached levels not previously experienced, meant beating inflation was no longer the main aim of the UK government policy in the 1980s. It has become a widely held view that a stable price level is a necessary precondition for the reduction of unemployment and the promotion of economic growth. As Nigel Lawson, Chancellor of the Exchequer from 1983 to 1989, put it:

> *'We set as the overriding objective of macroeconomic policy the conquest of inflation.'*

In this chapter we shall examine in more detail what is meant by inflation. First we look at the role of the **price mechanism,** which is how scarce resources are allocated in markets, and how it provides the necessary ingredients for inflation to come about.

The price mechanism

One of the major contributions made by economists, for a greater understanding of how our society works, is the analysis of the price mechanism. Largely as a result of the work of Adam Smith, we have come to see that if individual economic agents, workers, landowners, shoppers, investors etc., buy at the lowest prices and sell at the highest prices, then both they, as individuals, and society as a whole will be as well off as it is possible to be (in a material sense).

When there are shortages sellers raise prices, and this encourages suppliers to supply more and encourages buyers to look for alternative goods. When there are surpluses prices fall, which discourages suppliers and encourages buyers. Figure 1 shows the effects on prices and quantities of:

- an increase in demand from D_1 to D_2 with no change in the position of the supply curve;

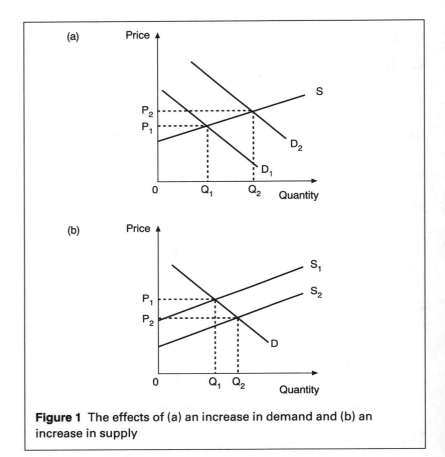

Figure 1 The effects of (a) an increase in demand and (b) an increase in supply

- an increase in supply from S_1 to S_2 with no change in the position of the demand curve.

What this demonstrates is that flexible prices are necessary for markets to work efficiently. Price fluctuations will signal to suppliers and to demanders where there are shortages and where there are surpluses, and they will adjust output in response to these signals.

In a dynamic, ever-changing, free-market economy we would expect prices to be always on the move – some going up and some going down and perhaps a few remaining the same. The price of fresh flowers on Mothering Sunday is two or three times higher than on the following day. All year, supermarkets cover their windows with information about price reductions and invite us to buy 'while prices are low'.

The price mechanism works by causing resources to be allocated to the production of certain goods. A change in the *relative* prices of two goods, say bread and potatoes, is enough to cause consumers to buy more of one and less of the other. Firms, in this case farmers, will alter the mix of products they produce in response to this price change. When firms and consumers are unable to tell whether prices are changing because of changes in demand and supply conditions, relative price conditions, or because of changes in the general price level, mistakes will be made and a misallocation of resources can occur.

The question that concerns us is: what is happening to prices *on average*? Relative prices must – and do – change, but relative prices are not our concern. We are here concerned only with their aggregate (average) behaviour.

Purchasing power

Many commentators believe that in the best of all possible worlds there would be no change in the general level of prices. Relative prices would be adjusted in such a way that each price rise would be exactly balanced by a price fall elsewhere. Achieving this exactly is unlikely, but the average price level will fluctuate, with these fluctuations evening out over time so that there is no long-run tendency for the general level of prices to rise or fall. What almost everyone wants to avoid is a sustained rise in the general level of prices.

To see what inflation means for those on *fixed incomes*, consider households with £100 to spend every week. They have to decide each week which are the best buys to put in their baskets. As relative prices change, the best buys change too, so goods whose prices have fallen are substituted for those whose prices have risen; but, on balance, with no inflation, the shoppers are as well off every week.

If, however, there is inflation (i.e. price rises are not compensated for by price falls elsewhere), then the shoppers become progressively worse off. As time goes by the £100 buys fewer goods.

This gives us another way of defining inflation: it is the *secular decline in the purchasing power of money*. With each successive year the pound is worth less in terms of the goods it can buy, and so inflation can be seen as a secular erosion of the value of the currency.

Table 1 shows how the value of the pound sterling – in terms of its ability to be exchanged for goods in the UK – has changed between 1920 and 1994.

Table 1 Purchasing power of the pound (1920 = 100)

1920	1925	1930	1935	1940	1945	1950	1955
100	125	135	157	129	111	98	76

1960	1965	1970	1975	1980	1985	1990	1994
66	56	46	27	13	8.9	6.8	6.0

Reading along the rows, we see that £100 in 1920 would buy fewer goods than in 1935, when you could buy half as much again for your £100 – i.e. £157-worth of 1920 goods. Average price level had therefore been falling over that period. Since 1935, however, the pound has lost value. By 1950, £100 would buy the same amount of goods as in 1920, and by 1994 £100 would buy only the same amount of goods as £6 would buy in 1920. Someone putting their savings under their mattress in 1920 would have lost about 94 per cent of the value 74 years later.

Pure inflation

Of course, inflation can occur even when there are no changes in relative prices. If the price of every good were to double, then *relative* prices would remain unchanged but the *aggregate* price level would double. The shopper would find that £100 would buy only half the quantity of goods and there would be no price incentive to switch from some goods to others. Inflation of this kind, let us call it **pure inflation**, has no role to play in the efficient operation of the price mechanism since there are no changes in relative prices to reflect relative shortages (or surpluses).

This leads us to the distinction between real values and nominal values. The **real value** of money is given by the goods and services it can buy. The real value of £100 halved when the price level doubled, while the **nominal value**, or money value, of the £100 remains the same. To allow a clearer picture of how values have changed it is common to report statistics in **real terms** – i.e. the nominal value is adjusted to take account of the effects of inflation. In Chapter 2 we show how this adjustment is made.

The rate of inflation

Until now we have considered increases in price level but have said nothing about how long it takes for these changes to come about. In what follows we shall be considering the rate of change of price level – the **rate of inflation**. Typically we shall be comparing the price level at one point of time with the price level one year later. This is what is meant by the year-on-year figure and it measures the annual rate of inflation for a particular 12-month period.

If price level doubled in one year then the annual rate of inflation would be 100 per cent, but if this doubling of price level took 35 years then the annual rate of inflation would be only 2 per cent. *It is the rate of change of price level which is of interest rather than the absolute change in price level.* Few shoppers would be too concerned at an annual rate of inflation of only 2 per cent but many would look askance at 100 per cent in a year.

Degrees of inflation

Aldcroft suggests that four degrees of inflation can be helpfully, if somewhat arbitrarily, distinguished.

- First there is **creeping inflation** which is persistent but at a low level – less than 10 per cent.
- Second comes **severe inflation** which occurs at rates between 10 and 100 per cent.
- Third is **galloping inflation,** at between 100 and 1000 per cent.
- Finally there is **hyperinflation** (greater than 1000 per cent a year) which gets so high as to lead to the destruction of the currency.

Hyperinflation

When there is hyperinflation the currency can be used neither as a medium of exchange nor as a store of value. The rate at which money is losing its purchasing power is so rapid that between someone receiving their wages and spending them the wages will have lost an appreciable amount of their value. No-one therefore wants to hold or use money. This applies equally to those who are selling and those who are buying. Shop-keepers are reluctant to sell (exchange their goods for money) when the value of the money is falling all the time.

After the First World War, hyperinflations occurred in Austria, Germany, Hungary, Poland and Russia. In Germany the price level rose by 100 *billion* per cent.

After the Second World War, hyperinflations affected China, Greece and Hungary. The worst case was that of Hungary where inflation reached its peak of 42 000 *thousand billion* per cent in July 1946. This resulted in an increase in price level in Hungary of 3.8 per cent with 27 noughts on the end. Russia suffered hyperinflation in 1990 as chaos followed the collapse of communism.

It is the experience of hyperinflation and its destruction of currencies – particularly in Europe in the first half of this century – which lies at the root of many people's terror of inflation. To them, inflation of any kind will tend to lead to hyperinflation and hyperinflation must be avoided at all costs. We look at this again later.

In the UK and in most developed countries it is clear that:

- There have been fluctuations in the rate of inflation, but almost all changes are positive so that the price level continues to rise – albeit at an uneven rate.
- All countries have experienced inflation.
- There is a very wide variation in rates of inflation among countries.

The phenomenon of inflation is therefore widespread, uneven, feared and in need of explanation.

KEY WORDS

Inflation	Rate of inflation
Price mechanism	Creeping inflation
Pure inflation	Severe inflation
Real value	Galloping inflation
Nominal value	Hyperinflation
Real terms	

Further reading

CSO *Retail Price Index Business Monitor MM23*, Feb. 94, HMSO, London.

Dictionary of Modern Economics, Penguin.

Heathfield, D., and Russell, M., Chapter 16 in *Modern Economics*, 2nd edn, Harvester Wheatsheaf, 1992.

Maunder, P., Myers, D., Wall, N., and LeRoy Miller, Chapters 8 and 28 in *Economics Explained: A Coursebook in A-Level Economics*, 3rd edn, Collins Educational, 1995.

Wilkinson, M., Chapters 1 and 2 in *Equity and Efficiency*, Heinemann Educational, 1993.

Chapter Two
Measuring inflation

'There are lies, damned lies and statistics.' Disraeli

To measure the annual rate of change of a price, we have to measure the price level at one point in time and measure it again 12 months later. A kilo of sugar, for example, may sell for £1.50 on 1 January 1996 and for £2.00 on 1 January 1997. The increase in price is therefore easily measured as 50p over the 12-month period. The annual rate of change of sugar price will then be given by change of price divided by the original price, 0.5/1.5 = 0.3333, or just over 33 per cent.

If the prices of all goods rose at the same rate then measuring inflation would be easy. Unfortunately there is rarely, if ever, an occurrence of such pure inflation. Typically some prices rise a lot, others rise only a little, some remain unchanged and others fall. The problem then is to measure the 'aggregate' price when there is no common behaviour among individual prices.

There is no ideal solution to this question but there are plenty of second-best solutions.

Cost of living index

One of the earliest attempts at measuring aggregate price changes in the UK was begun in 1914 with the object of measuring the cost of living of working-class families. That is to say, there was an interest in finding out by how much wages should be changed in order to allow workers to maintain their standard of living when prices were changing. If aggregate price level rose by 10 per cent, then the cost of living rose by 10 per cent so wages should rise by 10 per cent too. The appropriate **basket of goods** for such a purpose is one representing the purchases typically made by working-class families and, at that time, included basic items such as bread, potatoes and candles.

Retail price index

In 1947 the official cost-of-living index was replaced by a more comprehensive measure of aggregate price change – the **retail price index** (RPI). The RPI has become the basic measure of domestic inflation in the UK.

In order to compute this price index, the government set out to discover the expenditure pattern of a typical UK household via a large-scale *Household Expenditure Survey*. A sample of households throughout the UK were asked to report on how they spent their incomes, and from this information a typical 'basket' of goods was constructed representing the average purchases made. Changes in the cost of this basket are used to calculate the RPI. Since 1957 there has been an annual survey of some 7000 households (the *Family Expenditure Survey* or FES), and these surveys provide the basis for the basket underlying the RPI. These 7000 households exclude pensioner households where three-quarters of income comes from pensions, and the top 4 per cent of households by income.

The expenditure pattern is, of course, changing all the time. We no longer rely on candles to light our houses and offices, and rarely burn coal to heat them. We do, however, buy video recorders and compact discs which simply were not available when the index was started. The appropriate basket is therefore continually changing and we are faced with the problem of deciding what our basket should contain.

The solution is to keep the basket fixed for a year at a time but to revise the basket every year in line with changes in the pattern of expenditure. Thus the FES has to be carried out every year. The basket for 1995 comprised some 600 separate indicators and is shown in Figure 2. It is clear that our greatest expenditure is on housing and household goods, and this is followed by travel and leisure and then by food and catering.

If our total expenditure – the whole basket – is given the value of 1000 points, then expenditure on housing and household goods would constitute 353 points, travel and leisure would be 239 points, food and catering 198 points, alcohol and tobacco 109 points, and personal expenditure 101 points. These 'points' represent the relative importance of these items in consumers' expenditure and are called weights. The areas devoted to each item in the pie-chart reflect these weights, so that 'housing and household expenditure' is about three times as big as 'personal expenditure'. *The larger the weight the bigger the influence it has on the RPI.* Thus if the price of 'housing and household expenditure' (353 points) rose by 10 per cent it would have three and a half times the effect on the RPI as would a 10 per cent rise in the price of 'personal expenditure' (101 points).

Now we have the basket for 1995 we need information on the price changes of each of its elements. The RPI is intended to be a measure of how much aggregate price level has *changed* rather than a measure of the level of aggregate prices. Every month 150 000 price movements of some 600 types of goods and services in 180 towns and cities are monitored and combined into a single figure using the weights of the basket.

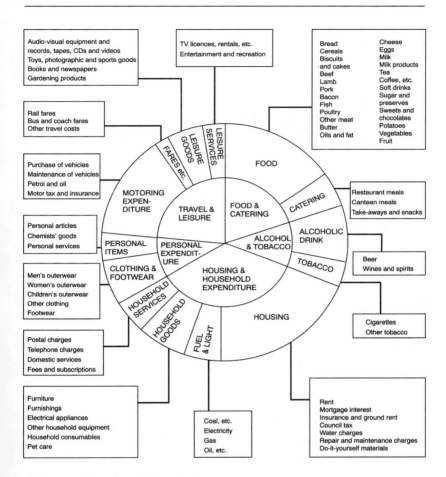

Figure 2 Structure of the RPI in 1995

These month-on-month changes in the aggregate price are the RPI.

The RPI therefore measures the monthly change in the value of a basket of consumer goods. The basket represents the expenditure pattern of a typical household and is updated every year to reflect the changing expenditure patterns over time.

These month-on-month changes can be linked together to provide comparisons of aggregate price levels between years. Figure 3 shows how the RPI has behaved since 1972. It will be evident from this figure that inflation – the rate of change of aggregate price level – has varied quite a lot, with the highest rate being over 25 per cent a year and the

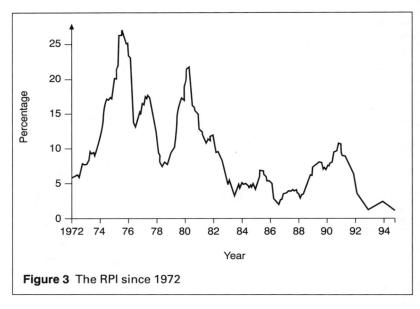

Figure 3 The RPI since 1972

lowest being less than 2 per cent a year. The aggregate price level never fell (or even remained constant) during those 23 years.

As its name suggests, the RPI is an index, and uses index numbers to express the price level rather than some average price. In the first year of the index, the base year, the index is set at 100. If prices rise by 10 per cent in the first year the index rises to 110, if prices rise by 10 per cent in the second year the *index* rises to 121 (*not* 10 points).

The monthly figures for 1994 and early 1995 in Table 2 show that the price index rose from 100 in January to 102.41 in May and June where it reached a short plateau before rising again fairly steadily upwards. These monthly figures allow us to compute the year-on-year inflation rate. For example, from February 1994 to February 1995 the index changed by 3.39 points, or about 3.37 per cent. The index for any month can be compared with that of the same month a year later to give the year-on-year, or annual, rate of inflation.

The annual figures indicate that in the 33-year period 1962–95 the 'cost of living' rose tenfold. What could be bought for 53p in 1962 would cost £1.00 in January 1974 and £5.76 in 1995! Another way of putting this is to say that the 'internal purchasing power of the pound' has fallen. In fact, by 1995 it had fallen to a mere 9 per cent of its 1962 value. It is called the 'internal' purchasing power because it shows what a pound would buy in the UK – it is not an indication of the purchasing power of the pound abroad.

Table 2 Change in the RPI from January 1994 (= 100) to February 1995

Jan	Feb	March	April	May	June	July
100.00	100.57	100.85	102.05	102.41	102.41	101.91
Aug	Sept	Oct	Nov	Dec	Jan	Feb
102.41	102.62	102.76	102.83	103.33	103.33	103.96

Sources: *Monthly Digest of Statistics* (various) and *Retail Price Index* (MM23), Feb. 1994

Is the RPI accurate enough?

The RPI is often used to justify demands for higher money wages. If inflation measured by the RPI is 4 per cent, wage negotiations often ask for compensation. State pensioners receive a rise in their pensions equal to the change in the RPI each year.

The RPI does not reflect the true change in the purchasing power of most household incomes. We have seen that pensioner households are excluded from the Family Expenditure Survey, and so the RPI 'basket' is influenced only by younger consumers. Pensioners often buy a different set of goods from working households, especially when considering housing costs – pensioners usually have no, or a very small, mortgage. When the rate of interest rises the RPI rises (just over a third of the RPI basket is housing and household expenditure), but a pensioner with no mortgage and some savings is probably better off.

Recall that inflation is defined as the sustained rise in the general price level. This has led some commentators to argue that the effects of changing council tax rates and interest rates should be excluded from the index since they are once-for-all effects which distort the real (secular) inflation rate.

This desire to exclude certain items from the index extends much further than excluding council tax and interest rates. Some economists argue that the retail price index will be erroneous because it reflects changes in VAT and petrol prices etc. These are determined by the government and OPEC and will be sharply changed from time to time according to circumstances and policies. Rarely will there be a persistent rise in any of these prices, and hence their influence on the retail price index should be excluded from any measure of the 'sustained rise in the general price level'.

An index that excludes mortgage interest rate, local council taxes and petrol prices is published. Since it is supposed to truly reflect inflation rate, it is called the core inflation rate or the **underlying inflation**

13

rate. To save any possible confusion, the full retail price index is now referred to as **headline inflation**. The following is a summary of various published measures of inflation:

- RPI is the retail price index based on the basket of goods shown in Figure 2.
- RPIX is the RPI without mortgage interest payments.
- RPIY is the RPIX without indirect taxes and duties (e.g. petrol duty and VAT).

Figure 4 shows how the RPIX and RPIY differ from the wider RPI definition.

Another type of price index is used, particularly in the construction of national accounts. These are known as 'price deflators' and relate to the whole economy. The Central Statistical Office (CSO) measures consumers' expenditure (in toto) in both current prices and in constant prices (e.g. at current prices and 1980 prices). Thus by dividing the

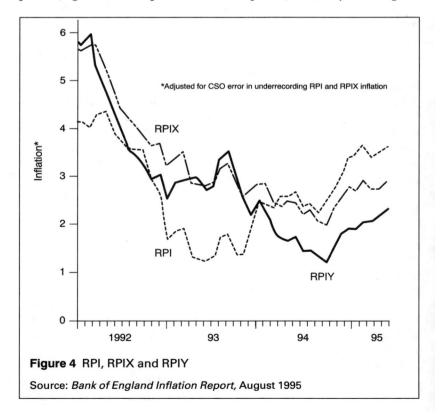

Figure 4 RPI, RPIX and RPIY

Source: *Bank of England Inflation Report,* August 1995

current-priced value by the constant-priced value we can get a measure of the change in the aggregate price level. This measure is called the **consumers' expenditure deflator**. It is the index by which consumers' expenditure at current prices has to be 'deflated' to arrive at consumers' expenditure at constant (1980) prices. It will differ from the RPI insofar as it includes all the expenditure by households rather than that of a 'typical' household. Thus the expenditures by the very rich and the very poor are included.

The **GDP deflator** is constructed in the same way, but includes *all* prices: it includes consumers', firms' and government expenditure. It is this index which is used to adjust UK national income statistics to *real* terms.

As can be imagined, there is much political interest in the construction and composition of these index numbers, and political parties tend to quote headline or core (underlying) inflation measures depending on which best supports their view of the world.

KEY WORDS

Basket of goods	Headline inflation
Retail price index	Consumers' expenditure
Weights	deflator
Underlying inflation	GDP deflator

Further reading
Anderton, Unit 93 in *Economics*, Causeway Press, 2nd edn, 1995.
Economic Review: Data Supplement (annual).
Heathfield, D., and Russell, M., Chapter 12 in *Modern Economics*, 2nd edn., Harvester Wheatsheaf, 1992.
'Measuring inflation', in *Economic Briefing No. 1*, HM Treasury, Dec. 1990.

Essay topics
1. (a) Explain how the rate of increase in retail prices in the UK is measured. [30 marks]
   (b) Why are there conflicting views as to whether the recorded rate of retail price increases provides an accurate picture of inflation in the UK? [30 marks]

(c) Explain why the rate of increase in the retail price index would be of much less concern than at present if the UK were a closed economy. [40 marks]

[University of London Examinations and Assessment Council 1993]

2. (a) How is the value of money measured? [12 marks]

(b) How substantial are the problems involved in measuring changes in the value of money? [13 marks]

[University of Cambridge Local Examinations Syndicate 1992]

Data Response Question

The shopping basket over 50 years

This task is based on a question set by the University of Cambridge Local Examinations Syndicate in June 1992. Study Table A and answer the questions.

Table A Data relating to the UK, 1939–1989

	1939	1949	1959	1969	1979	1989
Equivalent purchasing power of £1 then in today's money	£26.20	£13.20	£9.30	£6.60	£2.04	£1.00

(Prices below are expressed in new pence: 100 new pence = £1)

	1939	1949	1959	1969	1979	1989
Bread (large loaf 1½ lb or 800 g)	3.1	5.5	10.9	20.0	30.0	50.0
Beef (top quality) per lb	14.9	26.0	64.3	103.0	206.7	271.0
Bacon (back) per lb	15.8	31.0	58.4	76.9	115.9	162.0
Margarine (1 lb)	6.2	10.0	10.2	11.3	15.9	38.0
Milk (pint)	3.5	5.0	8.0	11.0	15.0	28.0
Butter (1 lb)	18.1	18.0	32.4	42.9	79.7	120.0
Cheese (Cheddar) 1 lb	9.9	14.0	40.7	42.4	86.9	144.0
Eggs (per dozen)	25.2	48.0	48.0	45.6	57.0	99.0
Sugar (white gran) 1 lb	4.4	5.0	7.7	8.9	33.1	57.0
Coffee (roast) 1 lb	25.8	*	90.0	115.0	221.1	135.0
Tea 1 lb	26.7	40.0	80.4	74.4	92.0	102.0
Beer (pint)	2.5	6.0	22.3	32.8	46.9	95.0
Cigarettes (20)	5.0	17.5	47.0	62.0	67.0	150.0

*Prices not given for coffee 1947–1955 owing to shortage in supplies

1. (a) How many pounds sterling were needed in 1989 to buy what the £ would buy in 1939? [1 mark]

(b) In which 10-year period was the rate of inflation greatest? Explain your answer. [2 marks]

2. Use demand and supply analysis to explain why the price of coffee behaved differently from all other commodity prices listed in the decade 1979–89. [3 marks]

3. Which of the items shown increased *most* in price over the whole period? Use demand and supply analysis to explain why this might have happened. [4 marks]

4. (a) To calculate a cost of living index it is also necessary to weight the items used in a typical shopping basket. Explain why this is necessary. [2 marks]

   (b) How would you expect the weight given to cigarettes to change in the future? Explain your answer. [4 marks]

   (c) Why would the way inflation is calculated be of significance to those who are retired and living on pensions? [4 marks]

Chapter Three

Costs and benefits of inflation

'Inflation is public enemy number one.'
Edward Heath, British Prime Minister, January 1973

Mistaken consensus?

Since Edward Heath spoke about inflation in 1973 it has been a generally held view that the conquest of inflation is the most important task for government economic policy. Whilst this view is beginning to be challenged in all political parties, the public universally see inflation as a *bad* thing.

Economists do not share the view of inflation held by the public. Inflation can be a good or bad thing for the economy, so we shall review the case for and against it.

Anticipated inflation

The problems caused by inflation can depend on whether it is expected or not. If everybody knows that inflation is going to be 10 per cent this year, and it is, then firms and consumers can plan for this. Such planning does not reduce the costs of inflation to nothing, but they are very small for the moderate inflation rates experienced in the UK.

Some economists refer to the menu costs and shoe-leather costs of inflation.

By the term **menu costs** is meant that, as inflation gets higher and higher, sellers have to revise their price lists. No doubt it will cost something to keep on reprinting these price lists, but even so there can be no case here for saying that inflation is a major, or even an appreciable, cost to the economy.

Shoe-leather costs can be explained as follows. With high inflation, the amount of cash we hold for day-to-day transactions is losing value all the time. If we take £400 out of an interest-bearing account, intending to spend it through the coming month, then an inflation rate of 1 per cent a month would mean that the last £20 (spent in the last week) would be worth 20p less than when it was drawn out. This would encourage people to go to the bank more often so as to leave their money earning interest for as long as possible. The time and effort spent making these journeys to the bank are the 'shoe-leather' costs.

Unanticipated inflation

● Confusion in the price mechanism

As we saw in Chapter 1, the price mechanism provides signals to firms and consumers on what to produce and purchase. When the price level changes due to inflation the price signals become confused. *The economic damage sustained during this transition arises from our inability to distinguish between changes in aggregate price level and changes in relative prices.* Thus if producers see that customers are prepared to pay more for their products (i.e. product prices are rising), should they interpret this as an increase in the demand for their products and increase their production, as the price mechanism would suggest, or should they assume that all prices and wages are changing by the same amount and thus their product is no more in demand than before?

What is being suggested is that inflation causes confusion by making it difficult for economic agents to perceive correctly changes in relative prices.

● Uncertainty

Unanticipated inflation gives rise to **uncertainty** about the future, so firms are unsure about the prospective real return on investment. The overall effect of this is to lower the level of investment in the economy, reducing the productive potential of the economy. Overall output may not fall, but the cost of lost output and unemployment is measured in terms of the level that could have been reached.

Consumers' confidence is also affected by inflation. If households are unsure how fast prices are changing they are unsure about the real purchasing power of their incomes. Their reaction is often to reduce purchases of real goods and services as their uncertainty causes them to be cautious. The result is a fall in demand for goods and services and a consequent reduction in output and employment. This means that we must either keep inflation low enough not to be an important consideration, or we must be extremely convincing in our forecasts of inflation.

● Income and wealth distributions

Some people feel that they have planned their lives carefully, saved, invested in pension schemes and generally acted responsibly only to find that the value of their hard-earned savings and pensions has been eroded by unforeseen increases in the price level. If price level doubles their pensions and savings lose half their value.

With regard to pensioners, it is quite difficult to find anyone on a

Why do people so often think in nominal terms? Perhaps because it is easier. Yet nominal thinking leads to bad decisions. That is awkward for governments trying to devise a policy on, say, controlling inflation. Low inflation makes money illusion less costly in terms of misallocated resources, because nominal and real values are similar. On the other hand, high inflation may make it easier for real prices to change, as they sometimes must. (For instance, workers in an uncompetitive company may need to accept a cut in real pay; they may be more willing if it is disguised as a rise in money pay.)

Source: *The Economist,* 24 Dec. 1994/6 Jan. 1995

truly fixed income. Many pensions, including state pensions, are index-linked. If the retail price index goes up by 10 per cent, then the pensions go up by that percentage. That is one reason why the government is so keen to get an accurate measure of retail price inflation.

Those who fear that their savings will be eroded can equally be reassured. When inflation occurs, the interest rates on savings deposits rise to cover the loss of value due to inflation and to pay the normal interest rate too. Of course it is not possible *always* to keep interest rates absolutely in line with inflation but, by and large, if the price mechanism is working properly, there should be no loss of value of savings from this source.

There are important redistribution effects in certain circumstances. Lenders have tended to lose out to borrowers, because the money repaid by the borrower buys far less than when it was lent. Consider the example of a house bought for £5000 in 1968 with a 100 per cent mortgage over 25 years. By 1993 the homeowners had repaid £16 000; but the house is now worth £120 000, so the borrowers have clearly gained from the transaction. The lenders can try to protect the value of their capital by raising interest rates when inflation rises, but in this (real) example would have done better to buy the house themselves.

Another redistribution occurs between the young and the old. Older people tend to hold more assets dominated in money terms (e.g. building society accounts) and these will lose some value during inflation. The young, on the other hand, tend to be net borrowers and so benefit from inflation. Although retirement pensions are index-linked, earnings have consistently outpaced inflation, so those in work, the young, find their real incomes rising faster than the old.

● International competitiveness

A somewhat stronger argument for controlling inflation lies not within the economy but outside it. As the price level in the UK rises, UK goods become more and more expensive. In other countries, too, prices may be increasing, but if the UK inflation rate exceeds the rates elsewhere then UK goods will become progressively less and less competitive *vis à vis* those other countries. This loss of competitiveness leads to a loss of export sales and an increase in imports. The demand for UK goods declines both at home and abroad, so UK workers are laid off and factories close.

This loss of competitiveness may be offset by a change in the **exchange rate** – the price of one currency in terms of another. If our exchange rate falls (devalues) at the same rate as our price level rises, then our goods will keep constant export prices and leave foreign demand for our goods unchanged.

In some circumstances the exchange rate has been determined by free markets, but this is not always possible. In Chapter 8 we shall see that at times the UK government has used the exchange rate as part of its anti-inflation policy and so devaluation is not possible.

● A strain on the market mechanism

It is possible that if the price mechanism is working well enough it can maintain relative prices at their 'correct' levels, revise interest rates so that there is no tendency to penalize lenders over borrowers, and correct exchange rates so that there is no loss of international price competitiveness.

This is placing a huge burden on the price mechanism, and many would argue that it is far too heavy. The price mechanism simply cannot keep up with anything more than very moderate rates of inflation.

Similarly exchange rates, even when they are free to float, are influenced by capital flows and expected capital gains as well as price level, and simply do not change to maintain our international price competitiveness. UK exporters complain that inflation therefore leads to their losing sales and/or profits to low-inflation countries.

- **Fiscal drag**

Our system of income tax is not designed for an inflationary economy. Typically the amount of income tax we pay depends on our nominal (money) incomes, and the amount of capital gains tax depends on the increase in the nominal value of our assets. Consider, for example, a tax system in which we pay no income tax if our annual income is below, say, £4000; we then pay tax at a rate of 25 per cent for the next £20 000 and then at 40 per cent for the rest. Income tax paid by some-one earning £60 000 per annum would be £19 400, which is 32.3 per cent of their income.

Now assume that inflation occurs and price level doubles. Incomes double too, so that the £60 000 becomes £120 000 – remember all prices have been doubled so the real value of this pre-tax income has not changed. The income tax paid now, however, will be £43 400 (check the calculation), which is 36.2 per cent of income. Thus the tax to pay increases simply as a result of inflation, with no change in the structure of tax rates nor our real pre-tax income.

The effect is more dramatic for low-income families. If the income before inflation were just £4000, then no income tax would be paid; but after inflation this £4000 would double to £8000 and there would be a liability for £1000 in income tax, and so the real post-tax income would have fallen by 25 per cent.

Of course, the Chancellor of the Exchequer receives greater and greater tax revenues as inflation proceeds – this effect is called **fiscal boost** – but not everyone would like to see greater public revenues at the expense of the poorer members of our economy.

To take account of the effect of inflation the Chancellor can change the amount people can earn before they pay tax. In most budgets the Chancellor raises the tax threshold by the rate of inflation or more, but there have been occasions when this has not been done, for example in November 1994.

Indexation

The changing of tax thresholds in line with inflation is known as **indexation**. Any price or value may be linked to a price index such as the RPI and adjusted in line with movements in the index.

If all prices, wages and values were fully index-linked then some economists argue that we could ignore the effects of inflation. For example wage negotiations could ignore the rate of inflation because wage rates would rise automatically. Instead they could concentrate on changing the real value of wages.

The required effort and cost of indexing all prices and wages would be considerable, especially if done frequently to avoid effects such as fiscal drag. Indexation could also obscure relative price changes, and so would not solve the problem of reduced efficiency in the price mechanism and it could also just build inflation into the system. It is argued by many that it is better and cheaper to keep inflation to a low level by economic policy.

Inflation: a good thing?

Some economists claim that mild inflation is positively beneficial to the economy. They argue that when we have some inflation it is easier for relative prices to adjust smoothly in response to market forces. This is because some prices and wages are very difficult to reduce in money terms. Trade unions resist cuts in money wages but seem to be less worried about cuts in real wages which come about when money wages rise slower than price level. Thus, when there is inflation real wages can be reduced without the need to decrease money wage rates.

To see how this works, consider a market that is signalling a surplus of lawyers and a shortage of accountants. According to our theory the salaries of lawyers should fall relative to those of accountants. It turns out to be quite difficult to persuade lawyers (and others in surplus professions) to take cuts in salaries. There are wage contracts and agreements which cannot easily be broken. But, if we had a mild inflation (say 3 per cent a year) we could gradually reduce the real salaries of lawyers by simply not compensating them for the inflation. Thus mild inflation actually eases the price mechanism.

KEY WORDS

Anticipated inflation	Uncertainty
Unanticipated inflation	Competitiveness
Menu costs	Exchange rate
Shoe-leather costs	Fiscal boost
Price mechanism	Indexation

Further reading

Heathfield, D., and Russell, M., Chapter 16 in *Modern Economics*, 2nd edn., Harvester Wheatsheaf, 1992.

Maunder, P., Myers, D., Wall, N., and LeRoy Miller, Chapter 8 in *Economics Explained: A Coursebook in A-Level Economics*, 2nd edn, Collins Educational, 1991.

Essay topics

1. Who gains, and who loses, from (a) inflation and (b) the effects of anti-inflationary policies? [10, 10 marks]
   [University of Oxford Delegacy of Local Examinations 1994]
2. Explain why inflation is regarded as a major problem for macroeconomic management. Discuss whether or not, in your view, zero inflation is a feasible or desirable objective for economic policy.
   [Northern Examinations and Assessment Board, Advanced Supplementary, 1993]
3. (a) What are the functions of money? [8 marks]
   (b) How are these functions affected when there is a large and sustained increase in the rate of inflation? [12 marks]
   [University of Cambridge Local Examinations Syndicate, Advanced Supplementary, 1994]

Data Response Question

Household expenditure

This task is based on an examination question set by the University of London Examinations and Assessment Council in 1991. Examine Table A, which is taken from *Social Trends* (HMSO, 1990) and answer the questions.

1. Explain what is meant by the phrase 'indices at constant 1985 prices'.
2. With reference to the table, which category of consumer expenditure shows (a) the fastest and (b) the slowest rate of growth in the period shown?
3. Outline the reasons, other than changes in real income, for these contrasting growth rates.
4. What does the table suggest about the income elasticity of demand for (a) food, (b) the purchase of vehicles, and (c) TV and video?
5. What is the significance of the changing expenditure pattern for calculating the index of retail prices?
6. What are the implications of the data for the changing pattern of employment in the UK?

Table A	1976	1981	1985	1986	1987	1988	£million in 1988 (current prices)
Indices at constant 1985 prices							
Food	96	98	100	103	103	103	36 687
Alcoholic drink	93	95	100	100	102	105	18 508
Tobacco	126	117	100	97	97	97	7 945
Clothing and footwear	67	78	100	108	116	122	19 791
Housing	84	92	100	103	107	111	42 993
Fuel and power	92	96	100	103	102	104	11 562
Household goods and services							
Household durables	81	85	100	106	109	120	9 711
Other	87	88	100	104	113	121	9 452
Transport and communication							
Purchase of vehicles	64	78	100	108	116	134	17 437
Running of vehicles	81	90	100	106	111	117	17 325
Other travel	82	92	100	106	118	127	9 986
Post and telecommunications	62	85	100	108	117	129	5 650
Recreation, entertainment and education							
TV, video, etc	55	72	100	114	123	133	6 413
Books, newspapers, etc	109	110	100	102	103	102	3 737
Other	82	94	100	105	113	120	15 946
Other goods and services							
Catering (meals, etc)	90	89	100	108	118	140	23 557
Other goods	89	86	100	107	116	127	12 292
Other services	57	73	100	112	126	133	14 999

continued on next page

25

Table A continued	1976	1981	1985	1986	1987	1988	£million in 1988 (current prices)
Less expenditure by foreign tourists etc. in UK	87	82	100	96	101	95	7 065
Household expenditure abroad	47	94	100	112	128	146	7 542
Total household expenditure	42	90	100	105	111	118	284 468
Percentage of total household expenditure at current prices							
Food	18.7	16.1	14.3	14.0	13.5	12.9	36 687
Alcoholic drink	7.7	7.4	7.5	7.1	6.8	6.5	18 508
Tobacco	4.2	3.7	3.3	3.2	3.0	2.8	7 945
Clothing and footwear	7.8	6.8	7.1	7.1	7.2	7.0	19 791
Housing	13.7	15.0	15.3	15.4	15.2	15.1	42 993
Fuel and power	4.8	5.1	5.1	4.8	4.4	4.1	11 562
Household goods and services	7.7	7.0	6.8	6.7	6.7	6.7	19 163
Transport and communication	15.2	16.8	17.0	16.7	17.2	17.7	50 398
Recreation, entertainment and education	9.3	9.4	9.4	9.5	9.4	9.2	26 096
Other goods, services, and adjustments	11.0	12.6	14.2	15.4	16.6	18.0	51 325
Totals	100.0	100.0	100.0	100.0	100.0	100.0	284 468

Chapter Four

Conflicting views on the causes of inflation

'Put all economists end to end and they would still not reach a conclusion.' Anon

The view of economists expressed in the quotation is often heard in the speeches of politicians and in the popular press. People usually want to be told 'the answer' and are frustrated either when no single answer is available, or various alternatives are offered. This problem arises in economics because we simply do not know exactly how some aspects of the economy work, and when economists form different views there is a debate, or controversy. The cause of inflation is one area of economics where there are strongly held, but opposing views.

The existence of a controversy makes economics a difficult subject for students because they are used to certainty – for example, nobody debates what force gravity exerts in A level Physics. Students of economics must be able to understand that there are equally valid alternative views in economics, and then be able to look at the available data. That is an important part of what economists do and it is a vital skill to learn. It is worth remembering that all the alternative theories may be wrong!

For those readers who are beginning to think that there is little point bothering with economics until we have sorted ourselves out, the following quotation gives an insight into the actual state of economic science:

> *'Academically, the discipline (economics) seems to have developed enormously. ... Of course, disputes still exist, such as the well publicised arguments between monetarists and Keynesians. ... But such tiffs conceal the large body of shared belief which characterises present-day economics.'*

Paul Ormerod, *The Death of Economics*, Faber & Faber, 1994

In this chapter we shall be looking at the *three main theories* put forward as the cause of inflation. In the next chapter we shall look at some of the inflation data for the UK.

Monetarist theories

Monetarists believe that the fundamental cause of inflation is an unmerited rise in the money supply. A merited rise in the money supply would occur if there was economic growth, for example. Professor Milton Friedman, who was the most public proponent of monetarism, is often quoted as saying:

'Inflation is always and everywhere a monetary phenomenon.'

The basis of the monetarist case is the quantity theory of money.

● The quantity theory of money

The **quantity equation** is expressed as:

$$M \times V = P \times Y$$

where M is the quantity of money in circulation, V is the velocity of circulation, P is the general price level, and Y is the quantity of real goods and services produced in the time period, usually one year.

The equation is more properly written as $M \times V = P \times T$, where T is the number of transactions. As the total number of transactions includes goods produced in previous periods – and the data on this are not available – economists usually use *current output* as an approximation. We shall use Y rather than T, but you may treat the two forms as similar.

The left-hand side of the quantity equation tells us how much money is in circulation (M) and how often each note or coin changes hands in each period – that is, how fast the money circulates, hence the term *velocity* (V). If there are 1000 £1 coins in circulation and each changes hands five times in the course of a year, then the velocity of circulation is 5 and $M \times V$ is equal to £5000. This tells us that firms, households and government expenditure has been £5000 during the year. Notice that doubling the velocity of circulation with the same money stock has the same effect on the price level as doubling the supply of money.

The right-hand side of the quantity equation tells us that the value of goods and services supplied is equal to the amount of real goods and services produced (Y) multiplied by the average price at which they are sold (P). In other words, $P \times Y$ gives us the money value, or nominal value, of national output. If the price level were to double then so would the money value of national output.

● From an equation to a theory

The quantity equation above must always be true, because it is nothing more than what is called an **accounting identity** – the value of expenditure on goods and services demanded and supplied equals the value of output. When looking back on a year the quantity equation must hold. The monetarist case is that inflation is caused by unwarranted increases in the money supply, and it is their assumptions about the quantity equation that make it a theory of the cause of inflation.

Monetarists assume that the velocity of circulation is fixed, at least in the short term. This is because the rate at which money circulates is determined by habit and institutional arrangements – for example how often workers are paid. The more often workers are paid the faster money could circulate. In practice such arrangements do not change very often, hence the assumption that V is fixed. In consequence any rise in the money supply cannot be offset by a fall in the velocity of circulation on the left-hand side of the equation, implying that the value of the right-hand side of the equation ($P \times Y$) must rise following a rise in the money supply.

Of course the rise on the right-hand side of the equation could be taken up by a rise in real output (Y). Monetarists rule out this possibility by assuming that real output is also fixed. Thus any rise in the money supply feeds directly through into higher prices, as the example below demonstrates.

Assume that the money supply is initially £1000 and the velocity of circulation is 5. The level of output is 5000 units and the average price level is £1. The quantity equation for this economy is:

$$M \times V = P \times Y$$
$$1000 \times 5 = 1 \times 5000$$

Now suppose that the money supply doubles. The velocity of circulation is assumed to be fixed at 5 and the level of output fixed at 5000 units. For the equation to balance the average price level must double (from £1 to £2):

$$M \times V = P \times Y$$
$$2000 \times 5 = 2 \times 5000$$

When the constraints of stable velocity and output are imposed on the quantity theory, the equation is known as the **Fisher equation**.

● **Introducing time into the quantity theory**
In fact monetarists accept that both the velocity of circulation and the level of real output do vary. The crucial points they make are that:

● velocity does not vary very much in *the short term* and can be treated as fixed, and
● real output can vary in the short run, but will return to a long-run

equilibrium level – sometimes known as **long-run supply** or the **natural rate of output** – quite quickly.

Thus in a short time any rise in the money supply will feed through into higher prices.

Milton Friedman himself suggested that the exact timing of the process will be difficult to predict, but gave a rough guide.

- Following a rise in the money supply there will first be a rise in the level of output around nine months to one year later.
- A further nine months to one year after that, output will return to its long-run equilibrium rate and prices will rise to accommodate the higher money supply.

Thus the entire process takes time and in the UK the monetarist view has often been represented as there being approximately a two-year *lag* between a rise in the money supply and a rise in the price level.

The process can be illustrated in the aggregate demand and aggregate supply model, which is debated in the article quoted from the *Independent on Sunday*. If you are not familiar with the workings of the model, refer to the further reading list at the end of the chapter.

- ## Monetarist inflation in the aggregate demand and aggregate supply model

Following a rise in the money supply, consumers will find they have more money available to spend and they will raise their demand for real goods and services. This shifts the aggregate demand curve to the right, from AD_1 to AD_2 in Figure 5. Firms will respond to this increase in aggregate demand and raise output, moving along the short-run aggregate supply curve, SAS_1 from A to B.

This rise in output causes the economy to exceed the long-run equilibrium level of output, given by LAS in Figure 5. What is known as an **inflationary gap** occurs, shown as IG in the figure. An inflationary gap is the difference between actual and long-run output when aggregate demand and short-run aggregate supply intersect to the right of LAS.

As a consequence of the rise in aggregate demand, from AD_1 to AD_2, firms hire more labour and work above normal full-capacity. As can be seen in Figure 5, this causes a rise in costs and so the average price level rises from $0P_1$ to $0P_2$. As prices rise, the quantity of money in circulation can buy fewer goods and services – a move to the left along the new aggregate demand curve AD_2. Furthermore, workers demand higher money wages in order to continue to work the hours required to produce the higher level of output, because higher prices have reduced the

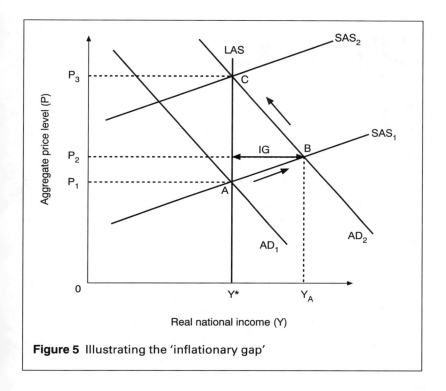

Figure 5 Illustrating the 'inflationary gap'

real value of their wages. The short-run aggregate supply curve moves to the left as money wage rates rise, to become SAS_2 at C. The economy gradually returns to the long-run equilibrium rate of output, but at a higher price level $(0P_3)$.

Notice that the rise in the money supply first caused a rise in demand; hence this form of inflation is known as **demand-pull** inflation.

The Keynesian view

Keynes rejected the monetarist view of how the economy works in his book *The General Theory of Employment, Interest and Money*, published in 1936. Keynes believed that the level of real output was determined by the level of aggregate demand, and that the price mechanism would not automatically bring the economy back to a long-run equilibrium level of output that was close to full employment.

In Keynesian theory, inflation is caused by excessive aggregate demand, as shown in Figure 6, but this is not due necessarily to a rise

31

Interview

MILTON FRIEDMAN

Milton Friedman has achieved a status sometimes found among pop singers or Middle East dictators, seldom among economists. He has become a hero, or a demon, in places he has rarely, if ever visited.

In Britain, a country he has only occasionally called on, his name still conjures up, depending on your viewpoint; the smack of firm government and the conquest of double-digit inflation; or rocketing interest rates, gross unemployment and the scything of swathes of British industry. He is unfailingly associated with the early Thatcher years, and with the M-word.

At his zenith, in the sixties and seventies, Friedman was the leader of the Chicago school of free-market economics, which prepared the way for Reaganomics and Thatcherism. (Eighty per cent of the economists in the Reagan administrations studied under Friedman.) Now, unlike John Maynard Keynes, he has lived, in the words of a younger US economist, 'to see his children die,' to see his ideas 'tried and abandoned and then disputed and mangled by the next generation of economists'.

Monetarism is not necessarily Friedman's most important contribution to the history of ideas, but it remains his most celebrated idea and, mangled and disputed though it may be, it refuses to go away.

His original conception of monetarism, he insists, was not applied properly in either Britain or the US. The plan was for governments, like Ulysses strapped to the mast, to set an unbreachable limit on monetary growth; in practice, in both London and Washington, he says, the politicians and bureaucrats could not resist interfering with the rudder. Instead of shrinking the supply in money directly (by restricting the supply of currency and credit to banks), the Thatcher government and the US Federal Reserve tinkered with interest rates – a Friedman no-no – in an attempt to achieve the same result.

The bureaucrats themselves and post-Friedman economists have a somewhat different memory. They say the theory was tried as well as it could have been tried; but Friedman over-simplified the difficulties of measuring and controlling the money supply. For Christopher Dow, Director for Economics in the Bank of England during the early Thatcher years, the very name of Friedman produces an audible intake of breath over the phone. 'Friedman had an unrealistic idea about how you could control the volume of money,' he says. 'He thought it was like a tap and you just turned it off. If you didn't stop the growth of money, you hadn't turned the tap far enough. The world doesn't work that way any more.'

The rising star of US economics today, Paul Krugman of the Massachusetts Institute of Technology, says: 'By the end of the 1980s, Friedman had made himself frankly ridiculous to professional economists. He was continually predicting outrageous inflation and severe slumps, based on monetary movements that strayed from his chosen path. And they didn't happen in the way he predicted.'

Friedman remains unshakeable in his faith that monetarism and the other free market experiments of the Eighties, in the US and Britain, did not fail: they succeeded in part but then fell back, through corruption of principle, or lack of nerve.

Independent on Sunday, 26 July 1992

in the money supply, but rather to the actions of firms, households and governments wishing to spend more than the economy can produce.

● Capacity output

Keynesians do not believe that the level of output in the economy is fixed. Rather they believe that it will fluctuate according to the level of aggregate demand. In an open economy, aggregate demand is the sum of consumers' expenditure (C), firms' investment expenditure (I), government expenditure (G), and the demand for exports less the demand for imports (X – M). A rise in any of these components of expenditure will shift the aggregate demand curve to the right.

There will be levels of aggregate demand that are not sufficient to employ all of the resources and workers in the economy, and so unemployment will result. At higher levels of aggregate demand the economy will have insufficient resources to produce the goods and services to meet this demand, and that is when inflation occurs. There is a level of output at which all resources are fully employed – this is the *capacity output of the economy* where there would be neither unemployment nor inflation. As the components of aggregate demand (C + I + G + [X – M]) are often determined independently, there is no

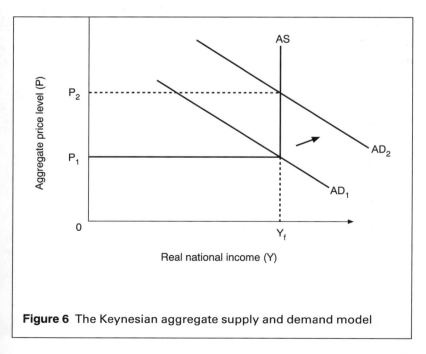

Figure 6 The Keynesian aggregate supply and demand model

reason why the level of aggregate demand should end up at the full-employment level.

In the simple Keynesian model, when the level of aggregate demand exceeds the real output of the economy at full employment level, the only way to accommodate extra aggregate demand is for prices to rise. In other words, the rise in price means the given level of aggregate demand can purchase fewer real goods and services. This is shown in the aggregate demand and supply model in Figure 6. The rise in aggregate demand from AD_1 to AD_2 means the economy moves on to the vertical part of the aggregate supply curve. Clearly any further rise in aggregate demand will lead to even higher prices.

- ● Inflation and unemployment

Figure 6 suggests that the price level remains the same until full employment (Y_f) is reached; i.e. there is only unemployment at levels of output below Y_f with no inflation. After the level of aggregate demand exceeds Y_f there is inflation and no further rise in output.

This is too simplistic a view, and all Keynesians would accept that there would be some moderate inflation before full employment is reached and the rate of inflation would rise as full employment is approached. The higher the level of aggregate demand the higher the rate of inflation. This is illustrated by the aggregate supply curve in Figure 7.

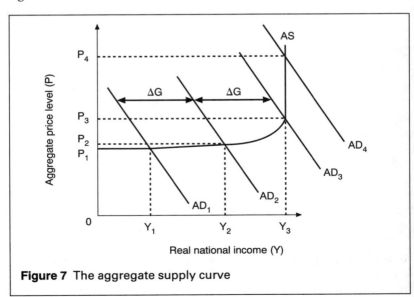

Figure 7 The aggregate supply curve

Figure 7 shows three shifts of the aggregate demand curve, the first two due to identical rises in the level of government expenditure (ΔG). In the first case, the shift from AD_1 to AD_2 causes both a rise in output and a fall in unemployment and raises the price level. The second movement of the aggregate demand curve causes a smaller rise in output and a larger rise in the price level. The shape of the supply curve has caused the difference between these two changes.

As real output rises the economy begins to run short of certain resources (perhaps skilled labour), and some resources such as machines run at full capacity. From microeconomics we know that, in the short run as output expands, the law of diminishing marginal returns sets in and firms' marginal costs rise. Thus as output rises towards full employment there is a slow rise in the price level as some resources reach capacity, causing a 'bottleneck' – a situation where a lack of capacity in one part of the system holds up preceding stages of production. The closer to full employment the economy becomes, the more bottlenecks there are in the economy and costs rise even faster.

Notice that after full employment has been reached in Figure 7, any increase in aggregate demand leads only to a rise in the price level and no change in output.

The Keynesians would, therefore, expect to see a strong relationship between the level of output and the rate of inflation. As output and employment of labour are so closely linked, the relationship between unemployment and inflation should be equally clear. Such a relationship was discovered by A. W. Phillips.

● **The Phillips curve**
Phillips found that when unemployment was high, wage inflation was low. As the economy expanded and unemployment fell, then wage inflation rose – slowly at first but faster and faster as unemployment fell further and further. This *nonlinear relationship* supports the view of the aggregate supply curve represented in Figure 7. The level of unemployment is a measure of how close the economy is to full-employment (capacity) output, and as this is approached so prices will begin to rise.

The **Phillips curve**, is in terms of wage rates and unemployment, *whereas we are interested in the causes of price inflation, not wage inflation*. The next step is therefore to forge a link between the money wage rate and the aggregate price index.

The link between the rate of wage inflation and price inflation is due to the large proportion of total costs of production made up by labour costs. If the wage rate rises, then firms will have to raise prices to protect profit margins *unless they can cut costs in some other way*. As full employment is approached, labour becomes more scarce and it is necessary to offer higher wages to attract the required workers. At such times the position of trade unions becomes much stronger and they may succeed in their attempts to negotiate higher wage rates for their members, free from the threat of unemployment. Even if a firm has a low proportion of direct labour costs as part of total costs, it will find the cost of inputs rising as its suppliers are obliged to raise their wage rates. These cost rises must be passed on to customers to maintain profitability.

The only relief for firms comes in the form of labour productivity gains. **Labour productivity** is a measure of the output per employee and this increases steadily over time. Any rise in productivity can be set against wage rises, and so the rise in the price level will be offset by a rise in labour productivity.

• Demand-pull again

The Keynesian view of the cause of inflation is also that it is due initially to a rise in aggregate demand. *However, the cause of the rise in aggregate demand and the process by which inflation proceeds differs from the monetarist view.*

The rise in aggregate demand is not necessarily due to a rise in the money supply, but any of the components of aggregate demand, and this leads to a rise in costs which are then passed on in the form of higher prices. The rate at which prices rise depends on how close the economy is to full employment, whereas in the monetarist case the rise in the money supply always leads to a rise in the price level.

The strong evidence provided by the discovery of the Phillips curve led to a widespread view that the Keynesian explanation of inflation was correct. As we shall see in the next chapter, in the mid-1960s the Phillips relationship seemed to have broken down.

Cost-push inflation

In many markets the degree of competition is insufficient to ensure a balance between suppliers and demanders, and market power plays a major role in the determination of wages and prices.

• Trade unions

An example of imperfect markets is the unionized sector of the labour market. Trade unions have many purposes, but an important aspect of their work is wage negotiations. Instead of each worker striking a bargain with an employer, a trade union negotiates for all its members together. Presenting a common front confers market power to workers, and so employers have to pay up or do without unionized labour altogether. Since labour, like oil, is a widely used and essential input into all productive enterprises, this increase in wages will force up costs and so force up price level too. The technical name for the market power being described here is **monopoly power**.

This view of inflation, based on the increasing market power of sellers, is clearly to do with costs increasing even when there is no encouragement to do so from the demand side of the market. It is therefore called 'cost-push inflation'.

● Commodity prices

Perhaps the best-known example of the influence of market power on prices is that in the market for crude oil. There being only a few big suppliers of oil, it became possible for them to collude rather than compete. Instead of each oil producer negotiating a price per barrel with oil users, the major oil producers and exporters formed themselves into a *cartel* in order to act in concert. This cartel is known as OPEC – the Organisation of Petroleum Exporting Countries – and together they fix a price for oil and present oil users with that price.

Thus there will be a rise in general price level whatever the level of the money supply or aggregate demand might be, as there was following the severe oil price rises of 1974/75 and 1979/80.

Although the prices of non-oil commodities do not have the same dramatic effect on inflation, any rise in their prices *can* feed through into higher retail prices.

● Cost-push inflation in the AD/AS model

When the costs of production in the economy rise – say, due to a rise in money wage rates – the short-run aggregate supply curve will shift upwards. *You will recall that in the monetarist and Keynesian theories the aggregate demand curve moved first.* The effect of a rise in production costs across the economy as a whole is shown in Figure 8.

Assuming that the economy begins in long-run equilibrium at real output $0Y_1$ and at a price level of $0P_1$, a general rise in production costs leads the short-run aggregate supply curve to shift to the left, from SAS_1 to SAS_2. This leads to a lower level of output, $0Y_2$, and a higher price level, $0P_2$.

Continuing inflation

The aggregate demand and supply model has, in each of the three theories we have examined, shown how there is a rise in the aggregate price level following a change in a key variable. *The model does not show continuing inflation, however – rather it implies a once-and-for-all rise in the price level to a new equilibrium.*

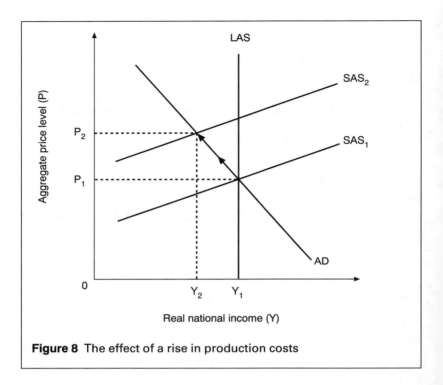

Figure 8 The effect of a rise in production costs

A once-and-for-all rise in the price level is not what we defined as inflation in Chapter 1. Inflation is a *continuous* rise in the general price level. The reasons why the price level continues to rise can be numerous. For example, there could be a sustained rise in the money supply in the monetarist case, or continuing rises in aggregate demand in the Keynesian case. In the case of cost-push inflation, the fall in real national output implies higher unemployment, and this may prompt the government to use fiscal policy – that is, cut taxes and increase government expenditure – to raise aggregate demand, further raising the price level.

The most common reason for continuing inflation is the effect a rise in the price level has on the behaviour of economic agents. This is often referred to as a **wage–price spiral**. The initial cause of the rising price level can be left aside; the effect of higher prices is to induce workers to ask for compensation in the form of higher money wages as they attempt to restore their previous real income. If they are successful, this leads to a further rise in the price level and further calls for higher money wages. The process continues as groups of workers try to maintain their relative positions in society – often referred to as maintaining **wage differentials** – where groups of workers try to maintain the same gaps between their wages and the wages of other groups, or their share of national income.

The response of the monetary authorities to a change in aggregate demand (a **demand 'shock'**) or in aggregate supply (a **supply 'shock'**) is also thought to be crucial. Suppose there is a rise in wage rates due to the ability of trade unions to negotiate wage rises higher than productivity gains. The aggregate supply curve moves to the left. The monetary authorities may decide to *accommodate* this supply shock by raising the money supply in order to restore real output, causing the aggregate demand curve to shift to the right and so the price level rises further. This **monetary accommodation** may be repeated for successive supply shocks – leading to continuous inflation.

If there is a demand shock – due, say, to a rise in autonomous consumption or investment – the aggregate demand curve shifts to the right. The monetary authorities may decide to *validate* this rise in aggregate demand by raising the money supply as the higher level of output and prices raises the transactions demand for money. This **monetary validation** continues the rise in the price level, and any compensating shift of the aggregate supply curve to offset the original demand shock fails to return output to its original level.

If a supply shock is not accommodated and a demand shock not validated, the rise in the price level will be a once-and-for-all movement and may even be reversed. *Thus the behaviour of the monetary authorities is vital in the path inflation takes.*

Inflation, once begun, can have many complex and interlinked reasons for continuing. It is far from easy to see the true cause during the process itself and to take action to halt the rise in the price level. For example, if the cause of inflation is due to cost-push factors, the money supply will still rise during this period in order to meet the demand for cash to settle the now-higher value of transactions, a rise in the transactions demand for money. Observing the money supply during this period may lead commentators to conclude that the cause of the inflation is due to the rise in the money supply.

The cause of inflation in the UK is a complex mix of many factors. In the next chapter we shall look at some data for the UK economy in order to discover more about the nature of UK inflation.

KEY WORDS

Monetarists	Labour productivity
Quantity equation	Monopoly power
Accounting identity	Cost-push inflation
Fisher equation	Wage–price spiral
Long-run supply	Wage differentials
Natural rate of output	Demand shock
Inflationary gap	Supply shock
Demand-pull	Monetary accommodation
Phillips curve	Monetary validation

Further reading

Anderton, A., Unit 94 in *Economics*, 2nd edn, Causeway Press, 1995.

Maunder, P. *et al.,* Chapter 14 in *Economics Explained*, 3rd edn, Collins Educational, 1995.

Parkin, M., and King, D., Chapters 23 and 30 in *Economics*, 2nd edn, Addison Wesley, 1995.

Essay topics

1. (a) Explain the possible causes of inflation. [12 marks]
   (b) Why have United Kingdom governments found it difficult to control inflation? [13 marks]
   [Associated Examining Board 1993]
2. 'Inflation is triggered by excess demand but sustained by rising costs.'
   (a) Explain this statement. [15 marks]
   (b) Discuss its implications for the control of inflation. [10 marks]
   [Associated Examining Board 1992]

Data Response Question

UK money and prices

This task is based on a question set by the University of Oxford Delegacy of Local Examinations in June 1995. Study Figure A and Table A, both of which are based on data from the *Annual Abstract of Statistics* (1994). Then use your knowledge of economics to answer the questions that follow.

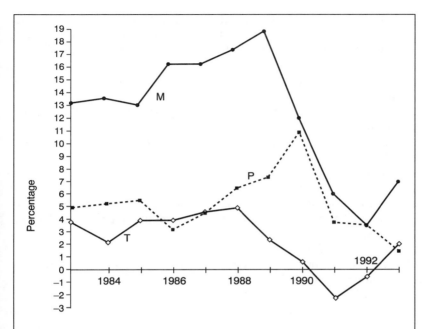

Figure A Rate of inflation (P) and percentage changes in money supply (M) and real GDP (T), 1983–1993

Table A Money supply and inflation (annual change)

Year	Money supply[1] (% change)	Inflation[2] (%)	Real GDP[3] (% change)	Velocity of circulation[4]
1983	13.2	4.9	3.8	1.8
1984	13.5	5.1	2.1	1.7
1985	13.0	5.4	3.9	1.7
1986	16.2	3.1	3.9	1.6
1987	16.2	4.5	4.6	1.5
1988	17.4	6.4	4.9	1.4
1989	18.8	7.3	2.3	1.3
1990	12.0	10.9	0.6	1.2
1991	5.9	3.7	−2.3	1.2
1992	3.4	3.6	−0.6	1.2
1993	6.9	1.4	2.0	1.2

Notes. 1: Money supply as measured by M4; 2: Based on the RPI (all items); 3: GDP at factor cost, at constant 1990 prices; 4: Measured on M4 basis.

1. (a) Examine the data on the money supply and inflation in Figure A and Table A, and discuss the extent to which changes in the growth of the money supply led to changes in the rate of inflation. [4 marks]

   (b) To what extent are your findings in (a) in accordance with economic theory? [4 marks]

2. (a) Examine the data on the money supply and real GDP in Figure A and Table A, and discuss the extent to which changes in the growth of the money supply are related to changes in real GDP. [3 marks]

   (b) To what extent are your findings in (a) in accordance with economic theory? [3 marks]

3. *On the basis of the information given,* why might it be difficult to predict the effects of an increase in the money supply on inflation? [5 marks]

4. (a) Suggest *three* items of data, other than that given, which would help you to obtain a clearer picture of the causes of inflation in an economy. [3 marks]

   (b) Briefly explain how a change in *one* of these items can affect inflation. [3 marks]

Chapter Five

Inflation in the UK

'We are all Keynesians now.'
Richard Nixon, when President of the United States of America, 1968

The breakdown of consensus

From the 1950s to the late 1960s it appeared that the Keynesian account of how the economy worked had provided economists with all they needed to know. When President Nixon uttered the famous words above, the economy had already begun to behave in a way that was inconsistent with the Keynesians' theory. In this chapter we look at the UK's experience of inflation and see how well the three theories examined in Chapter 4 conform to actual experience.

The breakdown of the Phillips curve

Faith in the Phillips curve, and in the Keynesian analysis of inflation, took a severe knock in the 1970s when very high inflation rates were experienced at the same time as there was very high unemployment (look ahead to Figure 10). Between 1967 and 1975 there was an enormous rise in inflation, from 4 to 26 per cent, with little or no change in unemployment. Since 1975, wage inflation has been variable but unemployment rates have been consistently higher than in the previous period. This conjunction of high inflation and high unemployment is called **stagflation**.

Stagflation is problematic for Keynesians because, if there is high unemployment there must be deficient aggregate demand; if there is deficient aggregate demand there can be no upward pressure on prices and wages; *therefore there can be no inflation: but there was.*

The decline of the popularity of the Phillip's curve was accelerated by the re-emergence of the monetarist view. Monetarists argue that the level of employment, and hence the level of unemployment, is determined by the level of **real wages,** which can be thought of as the amount of goods and services actual wages will buy. This means there can be no trade-off between unemployment and money wages. Their theory certainly leads them to this conclusion and, after 1974, there is some empirical support for them; but there remains the evidence of the original Phillips curve.

● **Expectations-augmented Phillips curve**

Once workers expect 10 per cent inflation they will want a 10 per cent increase in money wages just to maintain their expected real wages. In their wage negotiations they will need 10 per cent more just to keep worker-hours (employment) at last year's level. To get them to increase worker-hours they would have to be offered a 20 per cent increase in money wages. They would then discover that inflation rose to 20 per cent rather than the expected 10 per cent and their real wage would be what it was before.

The point is that the Phillips curve depends on what workers expect future inflation rates to be. If they expect no inflation then the relationship between employment and inflation will look like the original Phillips curve, but if workers expect 10 per cent inflation then the whole curve moves up by 10 per cent. If they expect 20 per cent then the curve moves up by 20 per cent.

These 'stacked' Phillips curves are called **expectations-augmented Phillips curves** (Figure 9) and are due to the work of monetarists such as Friedman.

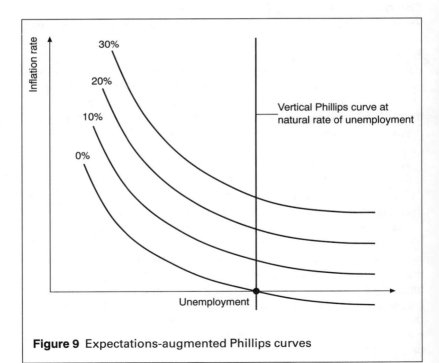

Figure 9 Expectations-augmented Phillips curves

● The natural rate of unemployment

As we have seen, employment is increased when workers underestimate inflation and is decreased when they overestimate inflation – that is what gives the Phillips curves their shapes.

If workers correctly estimated inflation – i.e. their expectations turned out to be correct – they would offer the *right* amount of labour and this *right* amount is called the **natural rate of employment**.The unemployment associated with it is called the **natural rate of unemployment**. Since this level of unemployment is the only rate compatible with correct expectations, all other combinations of unemployment and inflation rate must occur when expectations are wrong.

The Phillips 'curve' when expectations are correct is therefore a vertical straight line – often referred to as the vertical or **long-run Phillips curve**.

The vertical Phillips curve obviously occurs at the natural rate of unemployment, and the natural rate can be found by examining the data on unemployment and price inflation in the original Phillips curve. That curve was constructed when workers expected an inflation rate of zero. The natural rate of unemployment would therefore be that level of unemployment at which these expectations proved correct; that is to say, at that level of unemployment at which inflation would actually be zero. When actual price inflation is zero their expectations would be correct.

Whatever the level of price expectations, the rate of unemployment where expectations are correct is still the natural rate of unemployment. At all other rates of unemployment, workers either underestimate the rate of inflation when the rate of unemployment is less than the natural rate, or overestimate the rate of inflation when unemployment is greater than the natural rate.

If the level of unemployment is less than the natural rate, workers will demand wage increases higher than the expected rate to maintain the required supply of labour, and this will bring about a rise in the inflation rate. When the level of unemployment is above the natural rate, the rise in money wages demanded to keep secure the required amount of labour will be less than the expected rate and the rate of inflation will fall. *Only at the natural rate of unemployment will the required rise in wage rates match the expected inflation rate, resulting in stable inflation.* Thus another name for the natural rate of unemployment is the *non-accelerating inflation rate of unemployment*, or **NAIRU**.

● The Phillips curve 1965 to 1995

Figure 10 shows how the data on inflation and unemployment have

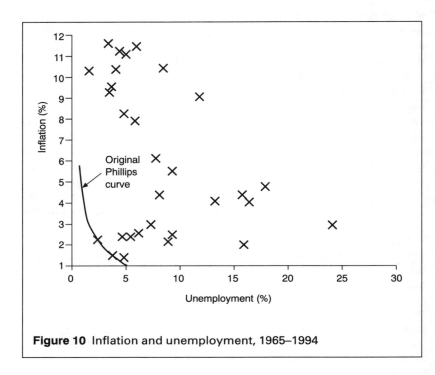

Figure 10 Inflation and unemployment, 1965–1994

departed from Phillips' original findings. This certainly does not support the simple Keynesian case for the cause of inflation, and the monetarist attempts to introduce expectations into the model seem to have some support.

The question of the existence of a natural rate is less easy to settle from the data. A natural rate helps the monetarists to justify their assumption about a fixed rate of output in the quantity theory, but none seems to be present. There have been various estimates of the natural rate of unemployment, ranging from 2.25 per cent in the 1960s to 12 per cent in the 1980s. In the 1990s it is thought to be 8 per cent.

Money supply and the rate of inflation

The monetarist case lies not with the expectations-augmented Phillips curve, but with the relationship between the money supply and the rate of inflation. In Chapter 4 we saw that monetarists expect a strong relationship between changes in the money supply and the rate of inflation, but with about a two-year lag. The relationship is defined by the quantity theory $M \times V = P \times Y$. In Chapter 4 we stated that monetarists assume V and Y to be fixed. *In truth monetarists relax the assumption of fixed real output in favour of allowing for economic growth.* The monetarist prediction is, therefore, that the rate of inflation will be equal to the rate of growth of the money supply (M) two years ago, *less* the percentage rise in output.

Figure 11 compares the rate of growth of broad money with the rate of price inflation. The evidence of the graph is mixed. In the period to 1981, a rise in the supply of money appears to be related to a rise in the rate of inflation. The evidence in support of the monetarist case is strongest in the early 1970s when very high rates of growth in the money supply were followed by high inflation a few years later.

The time lag involved appears to be highly variable, however. Let us take the period 1972 to 1974 as an example. The year 1972 saw a peak in the rate of broad money growth at 27.7 per cent. According to monetarist theory this should have led to a peak in inflation two years

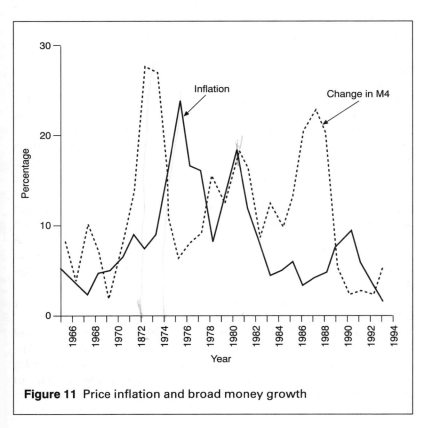

Figure 11 Price inflation and broad money growth

later, but the peak occurs in 1975, not 1974. Later, in 1980, inflation and the growth of the money supply peak together and thereafter the relationship appears to break down.

There appears to be some evidence of a link between the rate of growth of the money supply and inflation until 1981, but not in the exact way suggested by the monetarists. Further investigation is called for.

A closer look at the data

Figure 11 has not taken account of the change in output which must be allowed for when testing the monetarist case against the data. Let us take two periods and see how well the monetarist case holds using M4, the broad definition of money.

In the 1970s, the monetarists' 'two-year lag' did not appear to hold in this period, but the large rise in the money supply was followed by a large rise in the rate of inflation in subsequent years. The monetarists never claimed a precise time lag, and would argue that many other factors – such as changing exchange rates and government policy – would cloud the issue. Overall there appeared to be a strong link between inflation and the money supply in this period, and this had a major effect on the thinking of those who guided government policy in the 1980s.

Figures for the 1980s show that the relationship proposed by the quantity theory between the money supply and inflation had broken down in the later period. Very large rises in the rate of growth of the money supply did not feed through into inflation, although inflation did rise at the end of the period .

There is, of course, more than one measure of the money supply, and the quantity theory gives no indication of which would offer us the best guide to inflation. In fact, in recent years the favoured measure of the money supply has changed several times and several measures once reported have been abandoned and replaced with new ones. A key point is that the relationships between the different measures of the money supply have broken down, as Figure 12 shows. The different measures of the money supply have behaved in such different ways in recent years that the prediction of inflation each would provide from the quantity theory would be very different.

The data in Figure 12 show clearly that the behaviour of the different measures of the money supply are not consistent with each other. The very significant changes in the velocities of circulation of M0 and M4, in opposite directions, also suggests that assuming V to be fixed in the quantity equation is not valid.

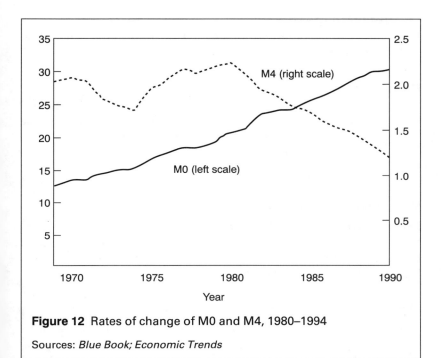

Figure 12 Rates of change of M0 and M4, 1980–1994

Sources: *Blue Book; Economic Trends*

Summing up

It would appear that neither the Keynesian nor the monetarist case on the cause of inflation can entirely explain recent experience in the UK. As a student you may find this rather frustrating, because there is apparently no conclusion to be drawn and the controversy continues. In itself this is a problem for policy-makers who need to understand the cause of inflation if they are to be able to form a policy to control inflation. The ever-changing nature of the economy means that past experience may be only a rough guide to the future. Evidently we are *not* all Keynesians now.

KEY WORDS

Stagflation	Natural rate of employment
Real wages	Natural rate of unemployment
Expectations-augmented	Long-run Phillips curve
Phillips curve	NAIRU

Further reading
Vane, H., and Thompson, J., Chapter 8 in *An Introduction to Macroeconomic Policy*, Harvester Wheatsheaf, 1993.

Essay topic
1. (a) Why is it considered important to control inflation? [10 marks]
   (b) Discuss how a government's commitment to achieve stable prices is likely to affect the level of unemployment. [15 marks]
   [Associated Examining Board 1994]

Data Response Question

Unemployment, inflation and savings
This task is based on a question set by the University of London Examinations and Assessment Council in June 1995. Study the data in Figures A–C and answer the questions that follow.

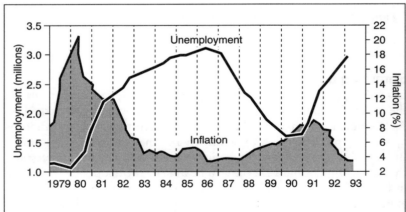

Figure A Unemployment and inflation

Source: *The Times,* 22 February 1993

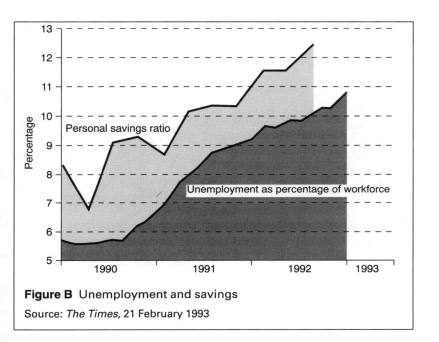

Figure B Unemployment and savings

Source: *The Times,* 21 February 1993

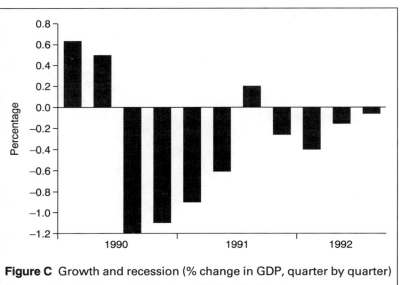

Figure C Growth and recession (% change in GDP, quarter by quarter)

Source: G. Cook, *Economics Update 1993,* Sterling Books

1. Using the data from both Figures A and B, estimate the size of the workforce at the end of 1992. Show your calculations. [3 marks]
2. (a) What does Figure A suggest about the relationship between inflation and unemployment? [3 marks]
   (b) Using economic analysis, explain the relationship you have identified in (a). [5 marks]
   (c) The Chancellor of the Exchequer said in May 1991 that unemployment was 'a price worth paying in order to achieve a low rate of inflation'. In the light of this statement, examine *two* benefits of a low rate of inflation. [4 marks]
3. Examine possible reasons which might explain the movement of the personal savings ratio between 1990 and 1992. [5 marks]

Chapter Six

The monetary system and financial institutions

The comparative neglect of the internal workings of the financial system contrasts with its significance for the conduct of monetary policy.

The importance of bank deposits in the money supply

It is generally believed that the sources of the money supply are the Bank of England and the Royal Mint. In fact the bulk of the money supply in the UK is made up of deposits in commercial banks and building society cheque accounts (we shall refer to all these institutions as the 'banks').

The extent to which money in bank deposits dominates the money supply can be seen from Table 3.

Table 3 The quantity of money in September 1995

M0	£22 817 million
M4	£607 865 million

- M0 is defined as notes and coins in circulation, plus money in bank tills, plus bankers' operational deposits at the Bank of England.
- M4 is defined as notes and coins in circulation, plus private sector sterling deposits (both interest and non-interest bearing) in commercial banks and building societies, plus sterling certificates of deposit.

M0 is the narrowest definition of the money supply reported and is clearly in the control of the Bank of England. M4 is currently the widest definition of the money supply reported.

The UK money supply defined

Above, just two measures of the money supply were used to illustrate the importance of bank deposits to the money supply.

In the past many more measures of the money supply have been reported. The reason for having more than one measure of the money supply is to allow the statistics to encompass all the various functions money is asked to perform. At the most basic level, money must act as both a 'medium of exchange' and a 'store of value'.

- The function of a medium of exchange is fulfilled by cash and access to cheques, which while they are not money themselves are a claim on money. Cash allows transactions to take place in the market and can be described as the narrowest definition of money in the economy. Hence M0 is known as a 'narrow' definition of the money supply, or in the terminology of the Bank of England the **narrow monetary aggregate**.
- The function of a store of value can be undertaken by many assets, not all of them acceptable as money because these assets are not generally acceptable in settlement of debt in general trading. There are many accounts that fulfil the store of value function that are classed as money, and these are included in the M4 definition of money. M4 is known as the **broad monetary aggregate**.

The tendency of our definition of 'money' to change presents economists and politicians with enormous problems – particularly those seeking to prove or use a relationship between money supply and inflation. It is clear that bank deposits make up a significant part of M4, and so we shall now look at how the banking system can expand the money supply by making loans ('extending credit').

Credit creation

Let us take the simple situation where there is just one bank in the economy. Let us further suppose that the bank, due to the law or good practice, always keeps a minimum of 10 per cent of its total liabilities in cash. This cash would be needed to meet the demands of depositors to withdraw money from their accounts each day. While there seems no reason for withdrawals to exceed deposits, remember everyone uses the same bank, there is no reason for the timings to match exactly.

If the Bank of England issues some new cash, this passes into circulation and is spent on consumer or investment goods. The firms that receive this revenue place some of the money in the bank and this gives the bank extra cash in its tills. The money, of course, belongs to the customer (the bank is liable to repay it at any time), but the bank knows that it is never likely to be called upon for more than 10 per cent of its total liabilities each day. The bank could then take 90 per cent of the newly deposited cash and lend it to another customer, and charge interest on that loan to make a profit.

This is not the bank's most profitable course, however. A better approach would be to keep all the cash in the bank and make a loan equal to nine times the size of the new cash deposit by simply crediting the accounts of borrowers. The bank has simply created the money it has lent to customers by writing it into their accounts and honouring all cheques and demands for cash withdrawals. The bank has maintained the required ratio of cash to liabilities at 1:10 (the customer's original deposit plus nine times the deposit as loans to other customers) and so will be able to meet all cash calls.

The ability of banks to create money in this way depends on the proportion of cash – or very liquid assets – they need to keep as a proportion of their total liabilities. If the proportion is 10 per cent then they can create 1/0.1, or 10 times more money for each new deposit. This is known as the **credit multiplier**. If the banks need only keep 5 per cent of their liabilities in cash then the credit multiplier is 1/0.05 or 20.

The significance of the credit multiplier

The description of the banking system in the last section is simplistic. Banks need to keep a range of interest-earning assets that are easily converted into cash – **liquid assets** – in order to allow them to operate freely. Banks are also required to maintain a capital adequacy ratio (banks' capital to total assets) and of course operate in a system with many banks. None of this invalidates the essential point that banks, given an expanding cash base, can create a great deal of money in the form of bank deposits.

At present banks are required to keep just 0.45 per cent of their total liabilities as cash. This implies a credit multiplier of 1/0.0045 or 222! From this analysis it should be clear that if a government wishes to operate a monetary policy it must be able to control – or at least influence – the ability of banks to create money.

The role and function of the central bank

Regulation of the financial markets is carried out through the **central bank**, which in the UK is the Bank of England. The Bank oversees the markets and tries to ensure good practice is maintained – this is known as its banking supervision role (the stock exchange and insurance markets have separate regulatory arrangements). The Treasury and the Bank constitute the 'monetary authorities'. The Bank has the role of managing the domestic monetary system and relations with other countries' monetary systems.

There are a number of important functions of the Bank of England that allow it to conduct monetary policy more effectively:

- *Issuing of notes and coins.* This allows the Bank to control the amount of cash in the financial system if it wishes.

- *Acting as the bankers' bank.* Each commercial bank maintains an account at the Bank. This can be used to control lending policy, as we shall see in the next chapter.
- *Acting as lender of the last resort.* The Bank will always ensure that banks have the necessary liquidity to meet their obligations to customers. However, the price (rate of interest) charged can be used for policy purposes.
- *Issuing and managing government debt.* The Bank raises any new loans the government requires and manages outstanding debt. For simplicity, assume government debt comes in three forms, cash, Treasury bills and consols. Cash and Treasury bills can form part of the liquid assets banks must keep to meet customers' requirements; consols are long-term bonds and so are not suitable as liquid assets. It is possible for the Bank to alter the structure of the government's debt and so alter the total amount of liquidity in the system. It is also possible for the Bank to influence market interest rates by the prices it accepts, or refuses to accept, for the sale of new bills and bonds.

This combination of roles allows the Bank of England significant influence within the financial markets – and so the ability to conduct monetary policy without the need for legislation, as is often required for fiscal policy. The ability to alter monetary policy in this way allows greater flexibility to the government, although monetary policy typically takes some time to influence the economy.

KEY WORDS

Narrow monetary aggregate **Credit multiplier**
Broad monetary aggregate **Liquid assets**

Further reading

Maunder, P. *et al.*, Chapter 18 in *Economics Explained*, 3rd edn., Collins Educational, 1995.

NIESR, Chapter 5 in *The UK Economy*, 3rd edn, Heinemann Educational, 1995.

Parkin, M., and King, D., Chapters 26 and 27 in *Economics*, 2nd edn, Addison Wesley, 1995.

Vane, H., and Thompson, J., Chapter 2 in *An Introduction to Macroeconomic Policy*, Harvester Wheatsheaf, 1993.

Essay topics
1. (a) Explain how commercial banks are able to create credit. [13 marks]
   (b) Discuss whether or not there are any effective limits to the amount of credit a bank can create. [12 marks]
   [Associated Examining Board 1994]
2. (a) Why is it difficult to find a satisfactory definition of the money supply? [8 marks]
   (b) Discuss the various ways in which the government and central bank can seek to influence the rate of growth of the money supply. [17 marks]
   [Associated Examining Board 1994]

Data Response Question

The credit 'problem'
This task is based on a question set by the University of London Examinations and Assessment Council in January 1993. Read the passage below, which is an extract from an article by Peter Lilley, then Economic Secretary to the Treasury, published in *Economic Progress Report* (HMSO) in October 1988. Then answer the questions that follow.

'Much has been said recently about the credit "problem". We should remember that borrowing is not necessarily a problem. Borrowing and savings are important economic activities, and we would all be worse off if they did not take place. Some people wish to bring spending forward on the basis of expected future income, and therefore borrow. Most people during their lifetime go through periods when they need to borrow and periods when they will want to save. They benefit from there being a free and efficient market in savings and loans.

The government takes seriously its responsibilities for prudential supervision and consumer protection in this area, on which much press comment has recently focussed. But there is only a "problem" for macroeconomic policy if total borrowing in the economy is growing faster than the growth in willingness of domestic and overseas savers to hold UK financial assets.

Where there is cause for concern about potential inflationary pressures, there are two things the government can do. First, it can borrow less itself. We have already done that. Indeed the government has moved from being the largest borrower to being the largest repayer of debt in the economy. Second, it can raise interest rates. The government has not hesitated to do so when necessary.

There has been a lot of talk recently about a further kind of action that it is said the government could take: to impose direct controls on credit. Even if this were desirable – which it is not – nowadays such controls simply would not work.

It is worth remembering the composition of consumer borrowing. Borrowing on credit cards, which catches the headlines, is only a tiny part of the total. Over 80 per cent of all borrowing by households is on mortgages (loans to buy houses). Only 15 per cent of personal sector debt is consumer credit. This figure includes credit cards, on which much attention focusses. But credit cards account for less than 5 per cent of the total.

And of that, credit card debt, a significant proportion is repaid quickly by the 40 per cent or so of credit card users who repay within the interest-free period, using credit cards merely as a convenient way of making payments.

So there would clearly be no point at all in seeking to control credit card lending only. To have any hope of having a serious impact, any control would have to cover mortgage lending also.'

1. What is meant by 'the credit problem'? [2 marks]
2. What is meant by the statement 'there is only a problem for macro-economic policy if total borrowing in the economy is growing faster than the growth in willingness of domestic and overseas savers to hold UK financial assets' [4 marks]
3. Analyse the effectiveness of the 'two things the government can do' where there is a concern about potential inflationary pressures. [4, 4 marks]
4. (a) What are direct controls on credit? [2 marks]
   (b) To what extent would you agree that 'such controls simply would not work'. [4 marks]

Chapter Seven

UK monetary policy in theory

'The overriding objective of monetary policy is price stability.'
Eddie George, Governor of the Bank of England, November 1992

The aims of monetary policy

Today, under the influence of the monetarists, the aim of monetary policy is generally agreed to be the control of inflation, as stated explicitly by the Bank of England. In previous periods, under the influence of the Keynesians, the aim of monetary policy was to influence the level of aggregate demand. These two periods cannot be precisely separated.

- During the earlier period of demand management, the direct controls of the money supply were typically employed.
- During the later period, inflation was the target and more indirect methods were used, usually working through the demand side for credit, via interest rates.

Directly influencing the money supply

The aim of directly influencing the money supply was to affect the level of aggregate demand. Figure 13 shows the effect of reducing the money supply in the **money market**. The money market is where banks and other financial institutions and large companies lend or borrow money, the sums involved are considerable and all transactions are settled on the same day. The fall in the money supply from MS_1 to MS_2 leads to a new equilibrium in the money market, and the rate of interest rises from $0r_1$ to $0r_2$. The rise in the rate of interest – which is the price of borrowing money – leads to a fall in the level of planned investment, as given by the investment demand schedule, from $0I_1$ to $0I_2$.

Investment is one component of aggregate demand, and a highly influential one. The fall in investment causes a fall in aggregate demand, and the aggregate demand curve shifts from AD_1 to AD_2. Notice that although the aim of the policy may have been to reduce aggregate demand and so reduce real national income, it may also affect the price level, which falls from $0P_1$ to $0P_2$ in the diagram, but this will depend on the slope of the aggregate supply curve.

This view of how changes in the money supply affect real output and

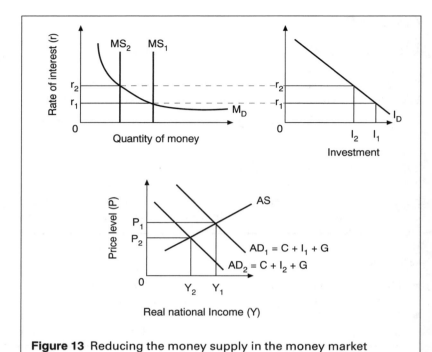

Figure 13 Reducing the money supply in the money market

the price level is a description of what is known as the **transmission mechanism** between the monetary and real sectors of the economy. The mechanism shown in Figure 13 is the Keynesian transmission

THE RATE OF GROWTH OF THE MONEY SUPPLY

The analysis here works by reducing the money supply and so reducing the price level. In reality no absolute reductions take place.

Monetary policy works by trying to reduce the *rate of growth* of the money supply and so *reduce the rate* of inflation. The theory presented here is limited by the tools of analysis available, and while these provide a useful insight into the aims of anti-inflation policy, they could mislead the reader into thinking that monetary policy was a simple matter of adjusting the key variable of money supply.

mechanism, which results in a lower level of output and a lower price level. The monetarist view, as outlined in Chapter 4, would suggest that the transmission mechanism between the money market and the price level is as outlined in the quantity theory of money. The fall in the money supply from MS_1 to MS_2 would, therefore, reduce the price level and in the longer term leave real output unchanged at the natural rate.

Both monetarists and Keynesians can agree on some of the effects of a rise or fall in the money supply, but not on how the effects come about. They also disagree on the extent of the effect the change in the money supply would have, and we shall look at this again later.

Techniques of directly controlling the money supply

The Bank of England had a number of possible tools of monetary control at its disposal during the period when it was felt feasible to attempt to control the money supply. Each was used with varying degrees of success. The first two methods relied on the existence of legally enforced reserve ratios and aimed to make use of the principle of the credit multiplier.

- ### Open market operations

The Bank could directly influence the cash reserves of the commercial banks through the buying or selling of government securities, such as consols and other long-term bonds, to the public in **open market operations**.

Suppose the Bank wished to reduce the money supply. It would offer for sale government long-term securities to the general public, who would purchase them by writing cheques that would be drawn against their own bank accounts. The Bank would present the cheques for payment to the purchasers' banks, which would settle the debts from balances they held in an account with the Bank. As these balances at the Bank of England form part of the commercial banks' cash reserves, a policy of selling government securities effectively reduces those reserves, causing a multiple contraction of the broad money supply. Purchasing government securities from the public has the reverse effect.

- ### Special deposits

A far more direct approach to reducing the money supply would be to take away cash reserves from the commercial banks, so forcing a multiple contraction of the money supply as they reduced their liabilities. This was the intention of **special deposits** and later supplementary special deposits, which are described below.

The Bank of England could simply call on the commercial banks to deposit part of their reserve assets with itself. Banks were not permitted to sell long-term securities to finance these deposits. Once deposited these balances, whilst still belonging to the commercial banks, could not be counted as part of the banks' cash or reserve assets. Special deposits paid no interest to the commercial banks and so represented a loss of income as well as preventing further profitable lending. They were often called for when banks ignored or exceeded lending guidelines issued by the Bank of England.

● Quantitative controls

Quantitative controls were used in the mid 1970s. Banks were told to limit their expansion to a certain percentage over each specified period. Exceeding the maximum permitted rate of growth meant the bank was required to place a percentage of the excess in a special deposit (a **supplementary special deposit**). The penalties were on a sliding scale, the further the permitted growth rate was exceeded the higher the proportion of the excess growth had to be deposited. Hence the system became known as 'the corset' as the larger the banks got the more the controls squeezed.

● Monetary base control

The monetarist school of thought suggests that controlling the money supply is crucial to the control of inflation. All of the methods described above were tools used by governments essentially convinced of the Keynesian view of the economy, and so were really aimed at supporting fiscal policy and influencing aggregate demand. The monetarist policy prescription is that the government adopt a 'monetary rule' and stick to it.

A suitable monetary rule might be *'the money supply will be limited to a growth rate of 4 per cent a year'*. If the trend growth rate of economy is 2 per cent a year, and if the rule is implemented, according to the quantity theory of money, inflation should average around 2 per cent over the medium to long term. This is not a policy that has ever been tried in the UK, but a number of suggestions have been put forward as to how it might operate, the best known of which is **monetary base control**.

The idea is to control the supply of **'high-powered money'** that forms the basis of the financial system's liquidity; this is mainly cash in circulation. If the amount of cash is restricted then so is the liquidity of the banking system, and so will be the ability of the banks to create credit. As the supply of cash is directly in the control of the government, the implementation of the policy should be achievable.

The principal objection to monetary base control is that interest rates would become volatile as attempts were made to keep the level of high-powered money within the required range. This would be destabilizing for the whole economy.

Influencing the demand for money

The demand for money depends upon a number of factors, such as income, expectations and the rate of interest. The monetarists contend that the demand for money is a stable function of the rate of interest and point to historical data to support their view.

So, argue some economists, why not simply change the rate of interest, causing a movement along the money demand function, and allow the money market to clear at this new rate of interest? Raising the rate of interest would raise the cost of borrowing and so reduce the demand for new loans. Banks would not be able to expand the money supply by extending as much credit as before, and so this would lead to a lower money supply – *or more accurately a slower growth in the money supply* – and would be an effective anti-inflation policy.

Control of interest rates

To be able to implement monetary policy via the demand side of the money market, it is necessary to be able to influence the rate of interest. This is certainly something governments claim they are able to do, but things are rather more complicated than they appear.

Often the news carries the headline:

> *'Bank of England raises base rate'*

This implies that the Bank can simply announce the rate of interest, but in fact it must take action to ensure the rate of interest really does move in the market.

The Bank has used the rate at which it will discount bills to the commercial banks as a way of influencing the short-term interest rates. Currently called **base rate,** this represents the official rate at which banks can obtain cash from the Bank of England.

This is just *one* interest rate paid on one type of asset, but there are many assets each with its own interest rate. These rates tend to move up and down in unison, so by raising the base rate the Bank can influence all other rates in the financial markets.

There are several other ways to influence interest rates, rather similar to those we have encountered for influencing the supply of money. Firstly, the Bank can reduce liquidity in the system by selling long-term securities in the market. This rise in the supply of long-term securities causes the price of securities to fall, raising the rate of interest paid on them.

Secondly, the Bank can restructure the national debt, moving the balance of debt away from the more liquid short-term bills and issuing a greater proportion of long-term bills. This can be done quite easily as Treasury bills have a life of only 90 days. When they are due for repayment, fewer Treasury bills and more long-term securities are issued in order to repay the holders, leaving the financial institutions with fewer liquid assets and again causing institutions to offer a higher rate of interest to obtain the use of the liquid assets they need.

A third alternative is simply to issue more government debt when the Bank wants to raise interest rates. The rise in supply of government debt will cause the price of government securities to fall, and this implies a rise in the rate of interest paid on those securities. *The price of a bond is inversely related to the rate of interest.* For example, consider a security that pays £10 a year to the owner. Ignoring the possibility of the security being redeemed (repaid), if the market rate of interest is 10 per cent then someone would be prepared to pay up to £100 to buy the security. £10 is 10 per cent of £100 and so represents a rate of return to the holder at least as good as they could get elsewhere in the market. If the rate of interest were 5 per cent, then someone would be prepared to pay up to £200 to obtain an annual interest payment of £10, being 5 per cent of the purchase price. *Hence when the interest rate goes up the price of securities falls.* As all other financial assets will need to offer a competitive rate of interest, their price will also need to fall; hence all interest rates follow.

There are grave doubts over the ability of the government to actually influence interest rates substantially, as we shall discuss in the next chapter.

Interest rate policies and the rest of the economy

Using the demand side of the money market to conduct monetary policy means changing interest rates. These have an effect on the real economy, just as directly controlling the money supply does. *Ironically the effect in the AD/AS model is identical to that of controlling the money supply.* If interest rates are raised the aggregate demand curve shifts to the left; if interest rates fall the aggregate demand curve shifts to the right.

Recall that aggregate demand is made up of various components, including consumers' expenditure (approximately two-thirds of GDP) and investment. Both are affected by changes in the rate of interest. If the rate of interest rises then it is more expensive to borrow. Fewer loans will be taken out by consumers, reducing household demand,

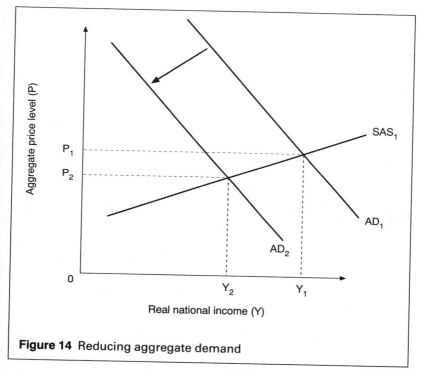

Figure 14 Reducing aggregate demand

especially for consumer durables such as cars, thus reducing the demand for real goods and services. Households will also find that they will have to repay more on existing loans, further reducing the available income to spend on current goods and services. This can be shown in the AD/AS model (Figure 14).

Following a rise in the rate of interest, we can expect the level of consumption and investment to fall. Both of these cause the aggregate demand curve to shift to the left, from AD_1 to AD_2, leading to a lower level of real output, $0Y_2$, and a lower price level, $0P_2$. Whilst clearly anti-inflationary, there is a cost in terms of lost output and employment.

The effect of higher interest rates on *investment* can be severe if the higher rates lead to a significant change in expectations. The quantity of new investment will fall owing to a movement along the investment demand schedule, or **marginal efficiency of capital** curve (MEC), but may also lead to a shift in the curve. Figure 15 shows the marginal efficiency of capital curve as quite inelastic, so there is only a small change in new investment from A to B due to the movement along the curve

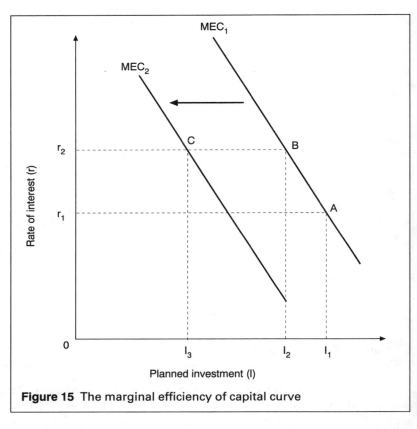

Figure 15 The marginal efficiency of capital curve

caused by the move from interest rate r_1 to r_2. If firms become highly pessimistic about future profitability and growth, they will be unwilling to invest even at lower rates of interest and the MEC curve shifts to the left, from MEC_1 to MEC_2.

This effect of changing interest rates is especially strongly felt through the *market for housing*. Where households have large outstanding loans, a modest rise in interest rates can lead to a substantial increase in monthly mortgage repayments as a proportion of monthly disposable household income. The combined effect of higher repayments and a generally lower level of disposable income caused by the rise in interest rates causes the demand curve for housing to shift to the left. In Figure 16, the supply of housing (Sh) is shown to be relatively price inelastic, because it is difficult to add significantly to the housing stock in the short term. A shift in the demand curve for houses, from Dh_1 to Dh_2, therefore causes the price of houses to change signifi-

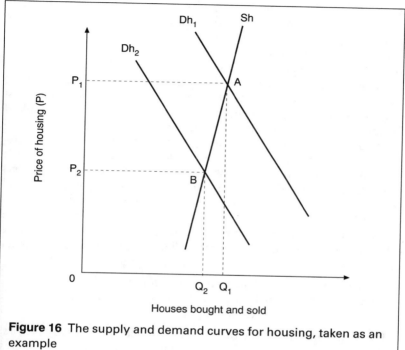

Figure 16 The supply and demand curves for housing, taken as an example

cantly. The period from 1989 to 1992 witnessed significant falls in the price of housing during a period of very high interest rates.

The *exchange rate* is also affected by interest rate changes. When the rate of interest in the UK rises relative to the rate of interest elsewhere, funds are attracted by the better return on sterling assets, and there is consequently a higher demand for pounds. This causes the exchange rate to rise and so exports become more expensive in terms of foreign currencies and imports become cheaper in the UK. This loss of competitiveness could lead to lower sales of UK-produced products, and so lower output and employment.

Time lags in the effects of policy

No economic policy has the full effect immediately that the policy-maker intended; all economic policies operate with a lag. It is possible to identify two types of lag, the inside lag and the outside lag.

The **inside lag** is the time taken for the authorities to implement a policy. There are often delays in data collection and in recognizing that there has been a permanent change in the direction of a variable such as inflation. Once policy-makers have decided that action must be taken, there is a further delay while the policy is implemented.

The inside lag of monetary policy is typically much shorter than the inside lag for fiscal policy. Changes in direct taxes and expenditure are announced annually in the budget and indirect taxes can only be altered by 10 per cent between budgets without Parliament's permission. Monetary policy changes can be made quite quickly, the Bank of England acting as soon as the decision is made.

The **outside lag** is the time taken to influence the targeted variables, i.e. the time the policy measures take to work through the economy.

It is helpful to distinguish between instruments, intermediate targets and targets at this point. An **instrument** is the variable over which the government has control and so changes to effect a policy change. Usually the policy instrument (say the rate of interest) does not directly affect the policy **target** directly (say inflation), but works by affecting other **intermediate variables** (intermediate targets) which do impact directly upon the target variable. A simple example is shown below:

Instrument:	*Intermediate variables:*	*Target:*
Rate of interest $\rightarrow$	Demand for money	$\rightarrow$ Inflation
	Money supply	

The length of time of the outside lag will depend on many factors, such as when the policy is implemented, other policy measures enacted, and so on. The difficulty of identifying turning points in economic variables and the length of time policy takes to affect the economy has led many to suggest that *precise control of the economy, known as fine tuning, is impossible.* Monetarists in particular believe that left to itself the economy will self-regulate and so all that is necessary is for policy to 'lean gently against the wind' rather than respond to every small change in direction.

KEY WORDS

Money market	Base rate
Transmission mechanism	Marginal efficiency of capital
Open market operations	Inside lag
Special deposits	Outside lag
Quantitative controls	Instrument
Supplementary special deposit	Target
Monetary base control	Intermediate variables
High-powered money	

Further reading

Barr, D., 'How the Bank of England controls interest rates', *Economic Review*, November 1995

Heathfield, D., and Russell, M., Chapter 18 in *Modern Economics*, 2nd edn., Harvester Wheatsheaf, 1992.

Parkin, M., and King, D., Chapters 27 and 32 in *Economics*, 2nd edn, Addison Wesley, 1995.

Shone, R., 'Monetary policy in the UK', *Sterling Economics Teaching Papers*. University of Sterling.

Vane, H., and Thompson, J., Chapter 9 in *An Introduction to Macroeconomic Policy*, Harvester Wheatsheaf, 1993.

Wyatt, G., 'Monetary policy and inflation', in Hare, P., and Simpson, L. (eds), *British Economic Policy*, Harvester Wheatsheaf, 1993.

Essay topics

1. (a) Explain how a significant rise in the level of interest rates in the UK might be expected to affect: (i) household spending decisions; and (ii) the general level of economic activity. [70 marks]
   (b) Discuss which sections of society gain and which lose from such a rise in interest rates. [30 marks]
   [University of London Examinations and Assessment Council 1994]

2. (a) How can the government influence the level of interest rates? [12 marks]
   (b) Discuss the likely effects of a significant increase in interest rates upon the rate of inflation. [13 marks]
   [Associated Examining Board 1995]

3. (a) How does the UK government seek to control interest rates? [8 marks]
   (b) Why might it wish to do so? [12 marks]
   [University of Oxford Delegacy of Local Examinations 1994]

Data Response Question

'One-way' economics

This task was set by the Associated Examining Board for the Advanced Supplementary examination in June 1994. Read the extract below, which is adapted from an article by John Grieve-Smith in *The Observer* in November 1991. Answer all the questions that follow.

One-way street to an economic dead end

Despite the undoubted success of Keynesian demand management in achieving full employment for the first 25 years after the Second World War, a generation has grown up that is in danger of adopting the inter-war attitude of fatalistic acceptance of mass unemployment.

This is partly attributable to the growth of the extreme doctrines of market economics associated with Hayek and Friedman, and which provided the intellectual content of Thatcherism, denying the ability of, or need for, governments to influence the economy.

In their extreme form, these ideas influenced, but never captured, finance ministries and central banks. Although 'demand management' became fashionable, in practice it remained inescapable. Any central bank or government has to take decisions continually on monetary policy, public expenditure and taxation, which affect demand. The truth is not that demand management has been dropped; but since the 1970s, the emphasis has shifted almost exclusively towards keeping demand down to fight inflation. The growth of 'one-way demand management' – a wayward offspring of the Keynesian revolution – is hindering discussion on how to get out of the recession.

The tragedy of one-way economics is that in the long run it makes high unemployment inevitable. After every downturn in the economic cycle, with its closures and bankruptcies, we are left with the ability to employ only a proportion of the labour force. Hence, when the economy does recover, inflation re-emerges at a relatively high level of unemployment. The Lawson boom was a vivid illustration of this. At the same time the balance of trade becomes more precarious as our manufacturing base contracts.

Given the problems of interest rate policy, the stimulus can only come from fiscal rather than monetary policy. There has, however, been a deafening silence about the use of such measures from all parts of the political spectrum. While one-way demand management holds sway, it is regarded as financially 'responsible' only to depress the economy, not to stimulate it.

Expansionary policies will however be possible only if we devise alternative means of tackling inflation. At present any recovery whether spontaneous or government-induced, is liable to lead to renewed wage-price spiral, unless there is a crucial change in present pay bargaining methods. The problem is that pay settlement that are acceptable to the two negotiating parties on their own, tend to be inflationary for the economy as a whole.

The persistence of mass unemployment in the 1990s would not only cause immense human suffering, but could once again pose a threat to European democracy, as it did in the 1930s.

1. Distinguish between monetary and fiscal policy. [3 marks]
2. Explain the difference between 'one-way demand management' and conventional Keynesian demand management. [5 marks]
3. Using the passage *and your knowledge of economics*, explain the mechanisms by which:

   (a) one-way demand management might lead to persistent unemployment, to inflation and to balance of payments problems; [7 marks]

   (b) expansionary policies might lead to a wage-price spiral. [5 marks]

Chapter Eight

UK monetary policy in practice

'The acid test of monetary policy is its record in reducing inflation. ...
The inflation rate is judge and jury.'
Nigel Lawson, as Chancellor of the Exchequer

The changing role of monetary policy
Monetary policy is just one component of overall economic policy.
The opinion of policy-makers on the role monetary policy should play
in general macroeconomic policy has changed significantly during the
period 1947 to 1995.

In this chapter we look at how monetary policy has actually operated. The operation of policy does not always conform to the theory
we have discussed, and so we shall trace out the frequent changes in
policy and try to explain why they came about.

The Keynesian era of monetary policy
We have already seen that the Keynesian explanation of inflation
rested on there being too much aggregate demand in the presence of
certain bottlenecks in supply. If the control of aggregate demand, via
fiscal policy, went beyond full-employment level, then there would be
an inflationary gap, and prices, rather than employment, would begin
to increase.

The view of Keynesians was that monetary policy was of little use. If
there was a rise in the money supply, Keynesians believed that any
excess would simply be absorbed into idle balances and not affect the
real economy. The standard opinion was that changes in the money
supply did not matter very much.

If monetary policy was used for domestic purposes, then it was used
to support fiscal policy in an attempt to influence aggregate demand.
In fact monetary policy was unavailable for most of the period
between 1947 and 1971 because the UK operated within a fixed
exchange rate system. The **Bretton Woods System**, as it was known,
required the government to keep the value of the pound sterling within
certain narrowly defined limits relative to the US dollar. If there was
downward pressure on the pound due to increased sales of sterling
(say because of a current account deficit), the Bank of England had to
buy pounds with foreign currency reserves in order to equate demand
and supply at the agreed exchange rate.

The net effect of this was that the domestic money supply decreased. *In this way money and monetary policy were constrained to maintaining the exchange rate and could not be used for domestic policy concerns.* This situation arose again during the UK's membership of the ERM between 1990 and 1992.

Anti-inflation policy in the Keynesian era

The discussion of direct controls of the money supply in Chapter 7 was mainly theory for the period before 1971. Anti-inflation policy was carried out by reducing aggregate demand through fiscal measures when an inflationary gap arose. There were two other anti-inflation policies employed in the period, although strictly neither comes under the heading of monetary policy. These were **prices and incomes policies** and **credit controls**.

● Prices and incomes policies

Through prices and incomes policies the government tried to change the shape of the Phillips curve. It tried to persuade workers not to take advantage of labour shortages by pushing up wages, and to persuade producers not to take advantage of excess demand for their goods by putting up prices.

This formed the basis of the various prices and incomes policies called the **Social Contract** by Harold Wilson. The 'contract', between the government and labour on the one hand and between the government and producers on the other hand, was that the government would increase aggregate demand so as to keep unemployment down to very low levels *provided* that no-one took advantage of the high level of demand to increase wages or prices. Voluntary or statutory guidelines on wage increases were issued, and if these were observed it would be possible to move the Phillips curve to a lower level of inflation at each level of unemployment.

Prices and incomes policies were ineffective and may be summed up as follows:

> '... *whilst some incomes policies have reduced the rate of wage inflation during the period in which they operated, this reduction has only been temporary. Wage increases in the period immediately following the ending of policies were higher ... and these increases match losses incurred during the operation of the incomes policy.*'

Henry and Ormerod,
National Institute Economic Review, August 1978

• Credit controls

Throughout the Keynesian period, the dominant theory put almost all the emphasis on controlling aggregate demand through fiscal policy. But some attention was paid to controlling credit. Typically this control was exercised on the credit households used for buying consumer durables. The controls were of two forms, the so-called 'down-payment' and the period of repayment. To borrow £100 it was necessary to already have, say, £10 or £30 to pay towards the good. To restrict credit the minimum amount required, as a percentage of value, could be raised, restricting the number of households that could now obtain credit. Shortening the repayment period made each repayment higher and so again reduced the ability of households to take up credit.

Credit controls were aimed at restricting aggregate demand, but acted on credit. Today the credit markets are international, *making such controls impractical.*

The era of 'money matters' and 'inflation first'

It is difficult to separate the Keynesian era from the period when monetarism first became the primary influence behind UK government policy. In 1976 a Labour government did introduce targets for the money supply and pursued policies that had as their aim the reduction of inflation at the expense of employment. On the election of Mrs Thatcher and the Conservative government in 1979, the top priority of policy had definitely switched away from unemployment to the control of inflation.

The Chancellor of the Exchequer in the first Thatcher administration (Sir Geoffrey Howe) spelt out monetarist policy in a budget statement in 1979:

> *'We are committed to the progressive reduction of the rate of growth of the money supply.'*

This was followed one year later by the advent of the **medium-term financial strategy** (MTFS), which set targets for money supply and the public sector borrowing requirement (PSBR) from 1980 to 1984. Annual increases in money supply were to be reduced from 7–11 to 4–8 per cent over that period. This pre-commitment of a four-year programme of slowing down the rate of change of money supply was to have two effects.

• First, its eventual implementation would reduce annual inflation rates according to the monetarist theory.

- Second, since everyone was to know what money supply – and hence inflation – would be in the medium term, they would avoid mistakes due to erroneous expectations of inflation.

This second effect depends largely on how convincing the government is. If we all believe it will actually meet the medium-term financial strategy, then we will form our expectations accordingly; but if we doubt the pre-commitment to the policy or the government's ability to carry it out, then we will form expectations as we always do – mistakenly. The policy of trying to influence expectations in this way can be seen in the context of trying to move the expectations-augmented Phillips curve downwards more quickly.

Thus the government tries to be convincing when it announces the MTFS.

Monetary policy and monetarist theory

The medium-term financial strategy did not directly control the money supply; rather it set targets for the growth of the money supply and the PSBR. This is not the monetary rule suggested by monetarists such as Professor Friedman (see Chapter 7). In fact, control of the money supply had proved almost impossible.

- The banks avoided direct controls by various methods, known collectively as **disintermediation**.
- The Bank of England always met demands for cash from the financial markets by discounting bills; thus attempts to restrict liquidity were ultimately frustrated by the Bank itself.
- The removal in 1979 of all **exchange controls** on the movements of funds between the UK and other financial markets meant it was just as easy to borrow 'in Dusseldorf as in Durham' and so controlling credit in the UK would be futile.

The money supply was, therefore, to be controlled by using interest rates, affecting the demand for money, and, as we shall see below, by controlling the size and funding of the PSBR.

In Chapter 7 we reviewed how raising the rate of interest reduces the demand for money. Figure 17 shows how the rate of interest has been manipulated frequently to achieve the desired monetary conditions.

The role of the PSBR seems more confusing. After all, the budget deficit is a tool of fiscal policy and so apparently outside the scope of a volume on monetary policy. There is a relationship between the PSBR and the growth of the money supply *which means that it is essential that fiscal policy supports monetary policy.*

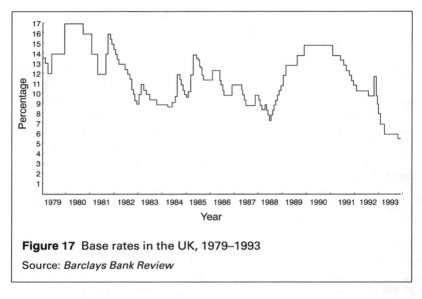

Figure 17 Base rates in the UK, 1979–1993

Source: *Barclays Bank Review*

Any lending to the government by banks will inflate the money sup-ply, because the banks will simply create the money they lend. However, if any part of the PSBR is financed by the private sector, by selling them bonds, then this does *not* add to the money supply. The PSBR and how it was financed legitimately became part of the MTFS and *fiscal policy became subservient to monetary policy*.

Funding

One method used to support the MTFS was **funding**, which technically refers to the replacement of short-term debt with long-term debt. In Chapter 7 we discussed how it was necessary to influence the market rate of interest in order to support announced changes in base rate. By funding, the Bank of England raised the quantity of long-term debt, forcing the price of such bonds down and so the long-term rate of inter-est up. This allowed the government to operate its high interest-rate policy to affect the demand for money. In the mid 1980s the Bank of England **over-funded** the PSBR – i.e. sold more long-term securities than was necessary – creating further upward pressure on interest rates.

From the mid-1980s until the 1993 budget, the government fully funded the PSBR. It issued new long-term debt to the full value of the PSBR (or bought back the equivalent amount of bonds when there was a public sector debt repayment). In this way there could be no cash creation, or 'printing of money' to finance the government budget deficit. The full funding rule was abandoned in 1993 because the projected PSBR of £50 billion for 1994/95 was thought to be too large to allow the issue of so many long-term securities without forcing interest rates up higher than the government wished to see them during a period of recession.

Monetarism abandoned

Around 1985 there was a subtle, but important, shift in policy. The government – whilst still publishing monetary targets – began using monetary policy to control the exchange rate.

A movement in the exchange rate has important effects on the competitiveness of exports and so has a direct effect on the real economy. The exchange rate is determined almost exclusively by the capital account of the balance of payments. With floating rates and no capital controls, the exchange rate moves to equalize rates of return on domestic and foreign assets, and quite considerable changes in the exchange rate and competitiveness are possible.

The government had realized that the exchange rate reacted to changes in the money supply. A rise in the money supply caused a fall in the rate of interest and this would cause an outflow of capital abroad. The exchange rate would depreciate to correct this, exports become more competitive, and so domestic production would rise. The higher level of real output causes a rise in the price level and a rise in the demand for money, which in turn causes a rise in the rate of interest. The overall effect of a rise in the money supply has been a *fall* in the exchange rate and a *rise* in the price level.

The aim of the new policy was to tie the pound sterling to the deutschmark. If the exchange rate could be maintained at a constant level this would imply that the two countries had similar monetary conditions (as there were no forces causing relative changes in their currencies' values). West Germany (as it was then) had a formidably good record on inflation, and so if the £:DM exchange rate could be maintained at a certain level the UK would be enforcing the same monetary conditions as the Germans and gain the same benefits of low inflation.

The tool of this monetary policy was to be interest rates, and whenever the exchange rate moved the Bank of England would have to manipulate interest rates to restore the desired exchange rate. Thus if the exchange rate depreciated, this would imply that monetary growth in the UK was higher than in Germany; to reduce monetary growth the rate of interest would be raised, money demand would fall, and the exchange rate would be restored.

The ERM

The UK entered the exchange rate mechanism (ERM) of the European Monetary System in October 1990. Essentially this is a fixed exchange rate regime in which the exchange rate of the pound for other European currencies has to be held within a plus-or-minus 6 per cent band around a central parity of £1 = DM2.95. Joining the ERM committed the UK to conducting monetary policy in a way that would maintain the exchange rate, which meant maintaining interest rates at the level indicated by movements in the exchange rate. The significance of this is two-fold.

- First, in a fixed exchange rate system the UK inflation rate must not exceed that of other European currencies. If it is higher it will reduce the UK's international competitiveness, so that excessive wage or price increases will lead to loss of orders, unemployment and so idle factories. In other words, *it is an externally imposed discipline on wage and price fixers.*
- Second, by committing itself to a fixed exchange rate the government increases the credibility of its anti-inflation stance. It simply cannot maintain a fixed exchange rate if it issues (or allows to be issued) too much money. *This is tantamount to saying that the government can either have a monetary policy or an exchange rate policy but not both.*

It was partly for this second reason that the more committed monetarists, like Mrs Thatcher and Sir Alan Walters, her chief economic advisor who described the ERM as 'half-baked', were so reluctant to enter the ERM. It meant giving up 'discretionary action to control UK money supply' – i.e. giving up monetary policy. To convince the markets that no devaluation would occur, both the government and the Governor of the Bank of England were emphatic in rejecting any such move.

After the ERM

On 16 September 1992, the pound left the ERM after massive speculative attacks meant the combined efforts of the European central banks were unable to maintain the agreed parity. The reasons for, and lessons of, the UK's experience within the ERM are discussed in Chapter 9.

After sterling's departure from the ERM the government was left in a quandary. Money supply targets had been abandoned in favour of an exchange-rate target, but now there was nothing. The solution, devised by Chancellor of the Exchequer Norman Lamont in the autumn of 1992, was to publish a target for inflation itself. The achievement of low inflation, after all, was the main aim of monetary policy.

The target was now to maintain underlying inflation within a 1–4 per cent range, with the added proviso that inflation should be in the lower half of the target range by the end of Parliament in 1997. The announcement of the target was accompanied by a number of institutional changes.

Every month the Chancellor would hold a meeting with the Governor of the Bank of England and senior Treasury and Bank officials. The meetings of this monthly committee would consider all the available evidence – the money supply, exchange rate, producer prices, house prices, earnings, world commodity prices and other factors. Everything would be taken into account in assessing the outlook for inflation. The minutes of these meetings were to be published to allow all to see how decisions had been arrived at.

Two other changes added to the Bank of England's influence:

- It was announced that the Bank in future would publish a regular, quarterly **Inflation Report**. The role of this report was to enable the Bank to publish its own inflation forecasts and to state publicly when it believed that inflation was likely to head outside the government's target range.
- The Bank was given control over the precise timing of interest changes, although only after a decision to change the rates had been taken by the Chancellor.

This system has been in place since 1992. The minutes of the monthly meeting between the Chancellor and the Governor are scrutinized for signs of future policy moves and disagreements between the Bank of England and the Treasury.

Disinflation remains the primary target, but the looseness with which all other targets are defined has allowed the government the luxury of ignoring poor money supply figures, or particular price index figures when it suits. The Bank of England has recently promoted debate on the use of inflation targets – such as what measure of inflation should be used and which inflationary 'shocks' can be ignored and which cannot. A recent reference to the discussion is given at the end of the chapter.

The era of 'inflation first' may be coming to an end as the government seeks to raise economic growth and encourage a revival in aggregate demand. We have been here before!

KEY WORDS

Bretton Woods system
Prices and incomes polices
Credit controls
Social Contract
Medium-term financial strategy
Disintermediation

Exchange controls
Funding
Over-funded
Inflation report
Disinflation

Further reading

Grant, S. J., and Stanlake, G. F., Chapter 61 in *Introductory Economics*, 6th edn, Longman, 1995.

Heathfield, D., 'Monetary policy 1947–91', *Economic Review*, May 1992.

Inflation Targets, Bank of England quarterly bulletin, August 1995.

Parkin, M., and King, D., Chapters 31 and 32 in *Economics*, 2nd edn, Addison Wesley, 1995.

Smith, D., *UK Current Economic Policy*, Heinemann Educational, 1994.

Vane, H., and Thompson, J., Chapters 10, 11 and 12 in *An Introduction to Macroeconomic Policy*, 4th edn, Harvester Wheatsheaf, 1993.

Essay topics

1. (a) What is meant by the money supply? [20 marks]
   (b) Why might a government wish to control the money supply? [40 marks]
   (c) Why is tight control of the money supply difficult to achieve? [40 marks]
   [University of London Examinations and Assessment Council 1995]

2. (a) Should control of the money supply be an essential part of macroeconomic policy? [60 marks]
   (b) Discuss *two* problems that have been encountered in the operation of monetary policy in the UK over the past decade. [40 marks]
   [University of London Examinations and Assessment Council 1994]

3. 'The public sector borrowing requirement will always rise in a recession and it is desirable that it does so.'
'The public sector borrowing requirement contributes to the rate of growth of the money supply and it is essential that it is strictly controlled at all times.' Discuss.
[University of Oxford Delegacy of Local Examinations 1993]
4. Explain what constitutes macroeconomic policy. Outline the broad changes which British macroeconomic policy has undergone since the 1970s and evaluate the success of the current measures.
[Northern Examinations and Assessment Board 1994]

Data Response Question

The Inflation Report
This task was set by the Oxford & Cambridge Schools Examination Board in 1994. Read the following passage, which is adapted from the Bank of England's *Inflation Report* in February 1993. Then answer the questions.

Inflation in the United Kingdom

The consistent message from a wide range of indices is that inflation has fallen sharply over the past two years. The decline was particularly rapid in those sectors most exposed to competitive forces, but there is also evidence of a substantial fall in the rate of increase of administered prices and prices with a high labour cost element. In the short run, changes in costs are a leading indicator of changes in prices. There was a marked slowdown in the rate of earnings increase in 1991–2; by contrast, cost pressures arising from the recent depreciation of sterling have been evident in the past few months, though producers may have scope in the short run to absorb such increases.

The government's inflation target is a range of 1–4 per cent for the rate of increase of underlying inflation. It is likely that inflation will remain in the 3–4 per cent range in the absence of any unexpected shocks. An outcome above 4 per cent in 1993 would reflect the impact of sterling depreciation on domestic prices. In the long run, competitiveness depends on real factors such as profit margins and real wages, and not on the nominal exchange rate. If labour costs and profit margins rise to offset the effect of depreciation then nominal retail prices will rise more rapidly than now looks likely. This would mean that underlying inflation might temporarily lie outside the target range.

The inflation outlook for 1994 and beyond depends on the balance between the continuing downward pressure on inflation resulting from the difference between actual and potential output, and the stimulus to inflation from past sterling depreciation and fears that part of the continuing fiscal deficit will eventually be monetised. The balance of probabilities is that inflation will be slightly lower in 1994 than it was at the end of 1992. The main risks to this prospect come from the possibility of a sustained further depreciation of sterling, a faster pass-through of the depreciation that has already taken place, and the effect of large fiscal deficits on expectations of future inflation.

1. Define (i) administered prices; (ii) leading indicator; (iii) underlying inflation; (iv) unexpected shocks. [4 marks]
2. What evidence would you look for to establish that there was a 'difference between actual and potential output'? Why should this put downward pressure on inflation? [4 marks]
3. Explain 'part of the continuing fiscal deficit will eventually be monetised'. [3 marks]
4. How might large fiscal deficits affect expectations of future inflation? [3 marks]
5. Discuss the relationship between a depreciation of sterling and the rate of inflation. [6 marks]
6. Why does the government have an inflation target? Evaluate its record in meeting it. [5 marks]

Chapter Nine

Looking forward

'In the 1960s we used to think that running the economy was like sailing an ocean-going liner, one touch on the wheel and you returned to the desired course. Now we know that running the economy is more like trying to cross the Atlantic in a dinghy with a handkerchief for a sail.' Alan Budd, HM Treasury

Monetary policy in the future

Since the departure of the pound from the ERM, the UK government has claimed that policy is guided by the desire to meet an inflation target of 1–4 per cent, and that inflation would be in the lower half of this range by the end of the Parliament (1997). The policy was outlined in Chapter 8.

It is difficult to see exactly what the guiding principles of policy are now. The monthly minutes of the meetings between the Chancellor of the Exchequer and the Governor of the Bank of England have revealed disagreement on priorities and action (see box 'Governor and Chancellor disagree').

European Monetary Union

The possibility of a single European currency has generated a huge amount of debate, much of it in the political arena. The economics of EMU are not one-sided and here we shall set out the conditions required and the pros and cons of moving the UK into a monetary union.

The Maastricht Treaty calls for the establishment of a single European currency by the end of the century. The time scale is unlikely to be met because certain conditions have to be fulfilled before a country can sign up for the single currency. The purpose of these conditions is to ensure that economic conditions within each country are broadly similar.

The conditions that must hold for each country, usually known as the **convergence criteria**, are:

- Inflation must not be more than 1.5 per cent above the average inflation rate of the lowest three countries.
- The national debt of the country must not be more than 60 per cent of GDP.

Governor and Chancellor disagree

The minutes of the monthly meeting between the Chancellor of the Exchequer, Kenneth Clarke, and the Governor of the Bank of England, Eddie George, are published some six weeks after the meeting. So far they have shown a lack of agreement between the two men over interest rate policy. Mr Clarke has been keen to keep rates low, while Mr George, worried about inflationary pressures, has wanted to raise them. At their May meeting Mr George stated:

'On the balance of risks, he (Mr George) was bound to advise that interest rates be increased by a half per cent now. If this did not happen, the authorities could be faced very quickly with a loss of credibility and a very difficult market situation.'

Mr Clarke replied that he was:

'... not convinced that interest rates should be raised that month. ... If interest rates were to be raised simply to match market expectations, then they could rise above the level required to meet the (monetary) policy objective.'

Mr Clarke stated that his view was based on a broad assessment of all economic data – implying that the market (and Bank's) view was too narrow.

- The PSBR must not be more than 3 per cent of GDP.
- The country's currency must have stayed within the narrow band of the ERM for a minimum of two years.
- The interest rate on long-term government debt must not be more than 2 per cent above the best three countries.

At the time of writing (October 1995), no EU country met all of these conditions. Many met none at all.

Arguments in favour of EMU
- *Transactions costs are eliminated.* Transactions costs occur when changing money from one currency to another. This must be done in order to do business abroad and so imposes an extra cost on traded goods. The argument is doubted by many, as wholesale costs of transactions are relatively small; it is only tourists (retail transactions) who pay a significant premium on their transactions.

- *There is increased efficiency in resource allocation.* The ability to exploit comparative advantage is enhanced when there are no exchange rates to consider. The existence of uncertainty over international transactions is present even in exchange rate regimes such as the ERM (as they can collapse within a day). Uncertainty limits trade, so reducing the full exploitation of comparative advantage.
- *With a single currency, monetary policy is in the hands of an independent European central bank.* The arguments for and against an independent central bank are discussed in the next section.

Arguments against EMU

- *The UK would lose the right to set monetary policy independently.* At present monetary policy can be set to deal with British problems. If the UK joined the EMU, monetary policy would be set in terms of Europe's interests as a whole. For example, if the UK lost competitiveness relative to the rest of the EU the option of devaluing the currency would *not* be available. In this situation the only policy open to the government is fiscal and micro – supply-side – policy. As fiscal policy can impact on the money supply this may not be fully available either.
- *Regional problems would arise.* In the initial period of monetary union, some areas would find that in the new open market they were uncompetitive and would experience rising unemployment. As discussed above, devaluation is not an option, and it will be necessary to institute **fiscal transfers** – the use of general taxation and government or EU spending in the affected regions – to cope with the problem. If such transfers are within present national boundaries there are unlikely to be significant problems. If the transfers are made between nations – for example from Germany to Portugal – there may be significant political obstacles and the problem will go unresolved.
- *The EU is not an optimal currency area.* The properties required of an **optimal currency area** require among other things the free mobility of labour and the ability to address regional problems. As it is difficult to see unemployed workers from Wales or the North East moving to Southern France or Greece where work is available, it is difficult to see the EU ever meeting the conditions of an optimal currency area.

The arguments for and against EMU will continue. They are arguments about monetary policy, but who or what institution controls it rather than what the monetary policy should be.

An independent Bank of England

Some commentators believe that the reason why inflation is tolerated by politicians is that the cost of reducing it in terms of unemployment and political unpopularity is too high. The problem may become particularly acute when elections near and the government is prepared to trade off some inflation for lower unemployment.

Arguments in favour of an independent Bank

- *Monetary policy operated at the discretion of the government does not work.* This is a view particularly strongly held by monetarists who would prefer a 'rule' to be adopted and followed. As governments often change their minds, an independent central bank with a legally binding charter to keep the price level stable is preferable to discretionary policy by government.
- *Fiscal restraint would be imposed on governments.* As we saw in Chapter 6, there is a link between the level of the PSBR and the money supply. If the central bank is pursuing a tight monetary policy, governments would be prevented from over-expansionary fiscal policies. This could equally be an argument *against* central bank independence as it is often argued that such restraint by unelected bankers is undemocratic.
- *Central bank independence raises the credibility of policy.* A major problem for the UK's membership of the ERM was that the financial markets did not believe that the government really would risk electoral defeat by raising interest rates to defend the pound. If monetary policy is legally prescribed and in the hands of an unelected body such as the central bank, then financial markets will have greater confidence in the policy being carried out regardless of circumstances.

Arguments against an independent central Bank

- *The chosen inflation goal may lead to a sub-optimal level of unemployment.* The central bank will form a view on the level of inflation that constitutes price stability, but the level of unemployment needed to achieve this may be more than the government (or the population) believe to be optimal.
- *Governments do not have the full range of policy options open to them.* The loss of monetary policy as a tool means that governments can use only fiscal policy, which we have already seen is not fully available, and supply-side policy. Some policy goals may be unobtainable with the available policy mix.
- *An independent central bank is unaccountable.* Once established

the independent central bank becomes unaccountable to Parliament. If the elected government wishes to change its mind about independence, it may be powerless to take back control. A more likely scenario is that the government and central bank disagree on the best course for policy and work against each other. The behaviour of the Bundesbank in the run-up to the ERM crisis in 1992 was interesting in that it pursued domestic goals and ignored the needs of other ERM currencies as they pushed up domestic interest rates to squeeze out inflation. The German government is strongly committed to the ERM and EMU, but could do nothing directly to redress the situation.

The evidence for the effectiveness of central bank independence as an anti-inflationary policy has received a great deal of attention recently. There is no clear relationship between central bank independence and growth.

KEY WORDS

European Monetary Union   Fiscal transfers
Convergence criteria   Optimal currency area

Further reading

Grant, S. J., and Stanlake, G. F., Chapter 64 in *Introductory Economics*, 6th edn, 1995.

Heather, K., Chapters 18 and 20 in *Modern Applied Economics*, Harvester Wheatsheaf, 1994.

Parkin, M., and King, D., Chapters 27, 31 and 35 in *Economics*, 2nd edn, Addison Wesley, 1995.

Scott, A., 'The European Community's impact on UK economic policy', in Hare and Simpson (eds), *British Economic Policy*, Harvester Wheatsheaf, 1993.

Smith, D., *UK Current Economic Policy*, Heinemann Educational, 1994.

Essay topics

1. 'Low inflation and low interest rates are the most important contributions that government can make towards industrial well-being.' Discuss.

[University of Cambridge Local Examinations Syndicate 1992]

2. 'Controlling inflation is easy. Controlling inflation whilst maintaining a high level of employment is impossible.' Discuss in the light of recent United Kingdom experience.
   [University of Oxford Delegacy of Local Examinations 1995]
3. How do you explain the fact that monetary targets are no longer the prime focus of economic policy in the UK?
   [University of London Examinations and Assessment Council 1993]
4. How convincing are the arguments in favour of granting independence to the Bank of England?
   [Oxford & Cambridge Schools Examination Board 1995]

Data Response Question

The Maastricht Treaty and EMU

This task was set by the Oxford & Cambridge Schools Examination Board in 1993. Read the article below, which is adapted from Andrew Britton, *From EMS to EMU; IEA: The State of the Economy 1992*. Then answer the questions.

Attempts to conduct an independent macroeconomic policy in Britain are now seen as a failure. A European monetary union, with a single currency, is now seen as the most reliable route to price stability.

The institutional framework for monetary union, as agreed at Maastricht, has been built mainly to a German model. The *proposed European central bank will be largely independent of government,* and therefore able to distance itself somewhat from political pressure. The over-riding aim of monetary policy, written into the constitution of the bank, will be price stability – i.e. a rate of inflation of about 2 or 3% a year. The Maastricht Treaty defines, precisely and arithmetically, just what *measures of convergence* are needed before individual countries are deemed fit to join a monetary union.

Clearly, any unified central mechanism must involve setting uniform interest rates. Indeed, the main instrument by which price stability will be secured will be the setting of these interest rates. Even in a monetary union, *the rate of inflation will not be identical in each country* and anxiety remains that the cost of achieving permanently low inflation will turn out to be very high for the countries with a history of relatively high inflation.

The case for monetary union rests on the belief that adjustments of imbalances between member countries is possible without changing exchange rates. Countries which become uncompetitive should reduce real wages or raise productivity so as to maintain or restore *full employment*. Within a nation state the problem of maintaining regional balance is solved in part by *fiscal transfers,* which help to narrow the regional dispersion of real incomes and employment levels. No such transfers are envisaged within EMU. The Treaty makes provision for some enlargement of the *regional and social funds,* but these are not designed to bail out the industries of countries which fail to reduce inflation and thus price themselves out of the European market. These funds will therefore do nothing at all to ease Britain's path to full membership of EMU. Now that exchange rates cannot move to compensate for lack of competitiveness, the main burden of adjustment must rest with wage and price flexibility.

1. Give *three* examples of 'attempts to conduct an independent macroeconomic policy in Britain'. [3 marks]
2. Define (i) full employment; (ii) fiscal transfers; (iii) regional and social funds. [3 marks]
3. What are the advantages of having a European central bank that is 'largely independent of government' [3 marks]
4. What is meant by 'measures of convergence'? Why is such convergence seen as a precondition of EMU entry? [4 marks]
5. Clearly, any unified central mechanism must involve setting uniform interest rates'. Why? [3 marks]
6. Why will the rate of inflation 'not be identical in each country'? [3 marks]
7. Why does the author believe that Britain's path to full membership of EMU might be difficult? What options are open to a government to smooth this path? [6 marks]

Conclusion

'Monetary policy has proved difficult to operate.'
Professor Sir Douglas Hague.

Professor Hague's words are, of course, an understatement. The period since 1971, when the post-war fixed exchange rate system broke down, has robbed the world monetary system of stability. The history of inflation and monetary policy since has been almost chaotic.

The Bretton Woods system gave the world a monetary standard. Money was linked to something – the US dollar. After the general floating of exchange rates, money was linked to nothing at all and, not surprisingly, the supply of money expanded rapidly.

The conflicting views on inflation we examined in Chapter 4 can perhaps be put into a longer-term context. The cause of rising prices in the short term may be due to any of the possibilities discussed, but a persistent rise in the money supply over nearly 30 years, which is not offset by a rise in real output, is bound to see a rise in the price level as predicted by the monetarists. The problem of running monetary policy in this period has been compounded by rapid institutional and techno-logical change both within the UK and internationally. It is no surprise, therefore, to see nations seek a new monetary standard such as the ERM or the single European currency.

At present the rate of inflation is not the acute problem it was, but this is partly due to a period of prolonged recession. There is no doubt that monetary policy will have to cope with numerous changes in Europe and quite probably rising inflation in the next few years. The one thing we can be certain of is that the policy response of the mone-tary authorities to the next bout of inflation or recession will be different from the policy responses of the seventies, eighties and early nineties. How can we be so certain? Because every policy response has been different so far.

Index